W9-ACG-067

THE PARADOX OF TRAGEDY

The Paradox
of Tragedy

THE MAHLON POWELL LECTURES
1959

—◦❦❦◦—

DAVID D. RAPHAEL

Essay Index Reprint Series

 BOOKS FOR LIBRARIES PRESS
FREEPORT, NEW YORK

PN
1892
R3
1971

INTERNATIONAL STANDARD BOOK NUMBER:
0-8369-2021-X

LIBRARY OF CONGRESS CATALOG CARD NUMBER:
77-128293

PRINTED IN THE UNITED STATES OF AMERICA

PREFACE

—◦⧱⧉◦—

These two essays form the substance of the Mahlon Powell Lectures which I was invited to give at Indiana University in the Spring of 1959. I should like to express to the Philosophy Department of that University, and especially to its Chairman, Professor Newton P. Stallknecht, my warm appreciation of the honour done to me by this invitation and of the kindness shown to me during my visit.

My subject is philosophy, not literary criticism, and the topics raised are dealt with as philosophical questions. My knowledge of drama is somewhat limited, and I am conscious that my appreciation of it may be biased in some respects by the strong impression made upon me in my youth by the Greek dramatists. Even of them I do not write as a classical scholar, but at least I have read most of the plays. With later drama, however, it is a very different story, and I can well believe that a more extensive and more detailed knowledge would require qualification of my views. My illustrations from post-Hellenic drama are pretty well confined to works written in English or French. Such acquaintance as I have with parts of French literature is largely due to my wife, and these essays owe much to her.

When using passages from Greek prose or verse, or from French prose, I have thought it best to borrow or give an English translation and, so far as practicable, to dispense with quoting the original language, though I regret the inevitable loss of beauty—in Anouilh as well as in Sophocles.

University of Glasgow   D.D.R.

CONTENTS

I. The Paradox of Tragedy

1

Why does Tragedy please?

WHY does Tragedy please? An old question, asked in the old-fashioned way. If someone objects that the alleged paradox of the pleasure of Tragedy is, like other old-fashioned philosophical problems, created by the language used, that one does not take *pleasure* in Tragedy as in a dish of roast lamb, let him substitute some other word. Why does one receive *satisfaction* from seeing the representation of misery? Why should one *want* to see a tragic drama? Not everyone does. But many people do, myself among them, and even rate the 'pleasure' or 'satisfaction' of Tragedy higher than that of any other *genre* of literary art.

Every schoolboy knows that our question was first answered by Aristotle. And every undergraduate knows that scholars and literary critics have drowned in an ocean of ink the laconic remark that Tragedy 'effects through pity and fear the *catharsis* of such emotions'. I do not propose to analyse or advertise the doctrine of *catharsis*. There is little doubt that Aristotle was speaking in medical terms. Some may find spiritual purification in comparing the mind to the bowels. I should prefer to see aesthetics purged of physiological criticism. Aristotle's *Poetics*, as we have it, is a fragmentary work, and we do not know what he had to say in detail about Comedy; but there is good evidence for thinking that he regarded Comedy, too, as some sort of purge. I am reminded of the therapy practised in Molière's college of doctors at the conclusion of *Le Malade Imaginaire*. Whatever the disease, the prescription is always the same:

> *Clysterium donare,*
> *Postea seignare,*
> *Ensuita purgare.*
> (With a clyster deterge,
> Then let the blood splurge,
> And finally purge.)

We may leave the physiological critics to give Aristotle the four cheers that Molière's doctors give to their neophyte:

> *Bene, bene, bene, bene respondere.*
> *Dignus, dignus est intrare*
> *In nostro docto corpōre.*
> (Jolly, jolly, jolly, jolly fine oration.
> He's fit, he's fit to take his station
> In our learned corporation.)

Aristotle's followers could hardly do less, since for them 'the Philosopher' was the infallible President of *their* learned corporation. It is enough to reply, with Mr F. L. Lucas,[1] that 'the theatre is not a hospital', and to follow him in quoting Fontenelle's bow to those Aristotelian doctors and the queer aesthetic digestions of their patients:

'I have never understood how the passions are purged by the passions themselves; so I shall say nothing about that. If anyone is purged by this means, good luck to him; still, I do not quite see what is the good of being cured of pity.'[2]

[1] *Tragedy*, London: Hogarth Press, 1927, p. 29.
[2] *Réflexions sur la Poétique*, xlv; original quoted by Lucas, p. 34.

Aristotle could have enlightened Fontenelle on the last point. The doctrine of *catharsis* is an answer to Plato's criticism of dramatic art in the *Republic*. Tragic drama calls forth pity for the distress of its heroes, and this, Plato thinks, will render us liable to self-pity, instead of endurance, when we meet misfortune ourselves. Pity is therefore antagonistic to virtue (as Plato understands virtue), and the attempt to control pity requires the banishment of the art that fosters it. Aristotle seeks to defend Tragedy while retaining Plato's criterion of justification. Harmful emotions must have some outlet; better to let them boil up at mere representations, and then the soul will be less troubled by them on real occasions of misfortune. Aristotle disagrees with Plato about the psychological effect of exciting emotion. In opposition to Plato's view (a sound one, in my opinion) that the capacity for emotion grows with exercise, Aristotle puts forward the specious doctrine that when our feelings are stirred we blow off steam and so are 'purged'. But he does not question Plato's ethical tenet that pity is a bad thing. The wonder is that men living in the tradition of Biblical ethics should have felt able to swallow Doctor Aristotle's medicine for the cure of compassion.

Plato speaks only of pity or sympathy. Why does Aristotle add fear? It is easier to answer that than to understand why so many people have accepted the addition. In his *Rhetoric* (Book II, Chapters 5 and 8), Aristotle regards pity and fear as near relations. It would be going too far to say that for Aristotle, as for Hobbes, pity *is* or always includes fear of similar calamities for ourselves (though when we criticize Hobbes, it is worth remembering that his error is simply an exaggeration of what he had found in Aristotle). Yet Aristotle does think, it seems to me, that one of the purposes of Tragedy is to make us fear for ourselves the distress we pity in others.[1]

It does not need much argument to refute the view that Tragedy is intended to arouse emotions concerning oneself. Classical and romantic tragedians alike place their characters at a distance of time, place, and status, in order to produce an impersonal contemplation. As someone has remarked, no member of Sophocles' audience was likely to suppose himself in any danger of murdering his father and marrying his mother through the extraordinary chances that brought such a fate to Oedipus. A modern playwright, Jean Anouilh, assures his audience that no disturbing emotions are stirred up by Tragedy; quite the contrary:

> Most of all, it's restful, is Tragedy, because you know that there is no more hope, dirty sneaking hope; that you are caught, caught at last like a rat in a trap. . . . And there is nothing more you can try; that's that![2]

[1] S. H. Butcher, in later editions of *Aristotle's Theory of Poetry and Fine Art*, is inclined to deny this (see 4th ed., London: Macmillan, 1907, p. 259, footnote on the phrase, φόβος δὲ περὶ τὸν ὅμοιον, 'fear concerns someone like ourselves', *Poetics*, xiii, 2). He says that, for Aristotle, 'the φόβος of tragedy is not, like the φόβος of the *Rhetoric* and of real life, a fear for ourselves'. He appears to overlook one passage in the *Rhetoric* (1383a8 ff.), which not only recalls the phrase, φόβος δὲ περὶ τὸν ὅμοιον, of *Poetics*, xiii, but seems plainly to compare the orator's representation with the tragedian's: 'When it is advisable that the audience should be frightened, the orator must make them feel that they really are in danger of something, pointing out that *it has happened to others who were stronger than they are, and is happening, or has happened, to people like themselves* (τοὺς ὁμοίους), *at the hands of unexpected people, in an unexpected form, and at an unexpected time.*' (Quotations in English from the *Rhetoric* are taken from the Oxford translation by Rhys Roberts. The italics here are mine.)

[2] First speech of the Chorus in Anouilh's *Antigone*.

16

He speaks with appropriate irony, no doubt, when he repeats, 'It's restful', but the disturbing effect of casting away all hope is not the disturbance of fear. Aristotle himself says that 'fear sets us thinking what can be done, which of course nobody does when things are hopeless'.[1]

Nor does it need much argument to show that Aristotle ties pity and fear too closely together. His doctrine rests on the fact that to be capable of pity we must be capable of imagining, and therefore of experiencing in ourselves, pain or evil such as that which we see affecting or threatening the person pitied. More generally, sympathy of any kind, since it includes the representation in imagination of another's feelings, presupposes experience of sufficiently similar feelings in ourselves. To pity another's pain I must know what pain is. But though the prospect of pain to myself will arouse fear, it is not necessary, for the experience of pity, that one should experience or imagine fear. It is enough to imagine pain and to possess what I shall vaguely call 'fellow-feeling'. Now this 'fellow-feeling' is referred to by Aristotle himself in *Rhetoric*, Book II, Chapter 13 (1390a19), where he throws out, in passing, a distinction between the kind of pity felt by the young and that felt by the old. The young, he says, pity others from '*philanthropia*', while the old do so 'out of weakness, imagining that anything that befalls anyone else might easily happen to them, which, as we saw, is a thought that excites pity'.[2] Aristotle recognizes here that the semi-selfish pity he has previously analysed is not the only kind there is, and we must agree with S. H. Butcher[3] that 'the tacit reference to self makes pity, as generally described

---

[1] *Rhetoric*, 1383a7.
[2] Cf. Butcher, *op. cit.*, p. 258, footnote 1.
[3] *Op. cit.*, pp. 257–8.

in the *Rhetoric*, sensibly different from the pure instinct of compassion, the unselfish sympathy with others' distress, which most writers understand by pity'. Having admitted that, we might as well discard altogether Aristotle's doctrine that Tragedy relies on pity and fear as he understands them.

Chapter XIII of the *Poetics*, which says most about pity and fear in Tragedy, also makes two references to *philanthropia*. Aristotle is discussing the kind of character, and the kind of reversal of fortune, suitable for a tragic hero. The spectacle of a wholly good man brought low from prosperity to disaster, he says, is neither pitiful nor terrible but only shocking. That of a bad man raised up from adversity to success has 'none of the necessary tragic qualities; it is neither "philanthropic" nor pitiful nor terrible'. The downfall of a bad man will not do either, for while it is 'philanthropic' it does not arouse pity or fear. There remains only the moderately good man, brought to disaster not by vice but by some *hamartia* ('error', 'fault'), and he, in Aristotle's opinion, is the ideal tragic hero.

Perhaps we should not attach any significance to the primacy of position given to *philanthropia* in the list of three emotions necessary for the tragic effect. Still, the fact remains that it is added as a third emotion. Aristotle evidently sensed here that his restricted form of pity was not enough; the appeal of Tragedy includes the evincing of a generous sympathy, which Aristotle could feel only when he was young.

I have not quite finished with Aristotle. I have dismissed *catharsis* summarily as old game, and have concentrated my discussion on the doctrine of pity and fear, which still seems to be accepted as a matter of course by many writers on Tragedy. I must now say something about *hamartia*, not from any thought that this part of Aristotle's theory has been insufficiently criticized by others, but in order to bring out farther the confusion in his account of the tragic emotions.

Aristotle distinguishes four possible subjects, and decides that only the last can be properly tragic. The first case, the downfall of a completely virtuous man, is rejected as unsuitable for Tragedy because it rouses neither pity nor fear but is shocking. One might well query Aristotle's conclusion about pity. (Fear certainly may be absent, but that is irrelevant, as I have already argued, and does not prevent the situation from being tragic.) It is commonly acknowledged that Aristotle is wrong to reject the downfall of virtue as a suitable subject for Tragedy. Both Antigone and Cordelia answer to it. Few of us will follow Hegel in judging Antigone morally culpable, or follow Gervinus in finding Cordelia to have been condemned to death by Shakespeare for the crime of leading a French army against England. We know that Dr Johnson 'could not bear to read the last scenes' of *King Lear* because he was 'so shocked by Cordelia's death', and preferred Tate's version with a happy ending. His experience confirms Aristotle's judgement that virtue come to grief is shocking. Let us leave that side of it for the moment. So far we have no sound evidence that this is not a fit subject for tragic pity, and we shall perhaps be more inclined to agree with W. Macneile Dixon[1] that the suffering of a blameless person is the *most* tragic type. Hegel indeed will not allow pity for Antigone, but then he will not allow pity for any tragic hero. Pity will do for your 'country cousins', he tells us; the heroes of Tragedy

[1] *Tragedy*, London: E. Arnold, 1924, p. 135.

are too noble for that kind of thing—and too Hegelian, for they recognize the justice of their fate. But Sophocles did not think so when he caused Antigone to make her final exit with the words, 'I have given reverence where reverence is due', as her verdict on her 'crime'.

One can see why Aristotle could not allow that the misery of a saint inspires fear. He says, a little later in the chapter, that fear is aroused by the misfortune of a person like ourselves. Since an audience is a collection of average men, not saints, they will not fear the misfortunes of saints. What of pity? This, he says, is aroused by unmerited misfortune; and the misfortunes of the saint above all answer to that description. I suppose Aristotle would hold, not unreasonably, that the moral offensiveness of the situation is too strong for any emotions other than shock.[1] The representation of virtue come to grief offends our moral sense. Aristotle is right enough about that. But we shall debar such a subject from Tragedy only if we are convinced, as Dr Johnson certainly was, that God does not allow such things to happen.

Let us now turn to the fourth case, Aristotle's ideal tragic hero, a moderately good man who falls into misfortune not through vice but through some *hamartia*. Unlike the misfortune of the completely virtuous, Aristotle seems to argue, the fourth case is not morally offensive, because the disaster is the result of *hamartia*.

If we do not share the ethical views of Aristotle and his masters, we may wish to deny this. The cause of the hero's downfall is expressly stated to be not vice or depravity but 'error', and where, we may ask, is the justice of that? Still, we have to remember that the *Poetics* was

---

[1] Cf. Butcher, *Aristotle's Theory of Poetry and Fine Art*, 4th ed., p. 309.

written by Aristotle, not by a Christian. Those who do remind us of this when discussing the doctrine of *hamartia*, too often take it unquestioningly for granted that Plato and Aristotle speak for all Greeks. Macneile Dixon, for instance, who is in general almost as hard as I am on Aristotle's theory of Tragedy, excuses Aristotle's mistaken doctrine of *hamartia* as typically Greek: 'For the clear-eyed intellectualism of the Greeks error was sin and sin error, miscalculation, in short, a form of guilt, for which Nature had no forgiveness.'[1] To be sure, the Greek philosophers Socrates, Plato, and Aristotle, all held an intellectualist doctrine of ethics. Virtue is knowledge, the perfect life is the philosophic life of knowledge. But I am not convinced that most Greeks agreed with them, and I am certain that the tragedians did not.[2] The tragedians would have agreed that ignorance can bring unhappiness, but does this imply that ignorance is sin? There is a difference between recognizing a fact and accepting it as just and proper. We have all heard of Margaret Fuller's decision to accept the universe, and of Carlyle's 'Gad! she'd better!' Not everyone does. Anouilh makes his tragic heroine one who says 'No', who refuses to accept the universe. The universe promptly crushes her, of course. She'd have done 'better' to say yes—better from a prudential point of view. But the tragedian perhaps is not concerned with the prudential view. He may, like Anouilh's Antigone, reject the way the world wags and the powers that wag it so. Euripides seems at times to take this attitude, and possibly Shakespeare when he wrote *King Lear*. Or the tragedian may, like Aeschylus

[1] *Tragedy*, p. 131.
[2] Cf. Macneile Dixon himself, for Aeschylus at least, on pp. 79–80 of his book.

and Sophocles, be merely puzzled and dissatisfied. What he does not do is to accept the world unquestioningly. Let us look a little more closely into Aristotle's preference for the erring hero. Does the hero's error justify his fate, even on Aristotle's view? *Oedipus Rex* seems to have been Aristotle's favourite Tragedy. Oedipus certainly suffers from *hamartia*, as Aristotle says. He is over-confident and over-rash, and his failings contribute to his downfall. But are they the main cause of his sins? Before he was born, the gods had doomed him to kill his father and marry his mother. They endowed him with his failings of character in order to carry out their plan, but even then all sorts of marvels and coincidences had to be contrived for the prophecy to come true. Even if he is held responsible for his defects of character and knowledge, can we apply Plato's dictum,[1] 'The responsibility rests on his choice; Heaven is not to blame'? Oedipus did not choose; he was pushed into it. Much the same is true of the *hamartiae* of other tragic heroes. Aristotle is not justified in saying that the misfortune is the *consequence* of *hamartia* in such a sense as to take away any moral offensiveness from the hero's fate.

Besides, if the hero did deserve his fate, he could not, on Aristotle's view, be the subject of pity. For, it will be remembered, Aristotle insists that pity is aroused by *unmerited* misfortune. If, therefore, a hero's misfortune arises from *hamartia* and so does not shock the moral sense as would the misfortunes of the virtuous, it is not unmerited and so cannot arouse pity. If pity is justified, the hero's *hamartia* does not prevent his fate from being unmerited and thereby shocking the moral sense. Aristotle cannot have it both ways: if *hamartia* is responsible,

[1] *Republic*, Book X, 617c.

there cannot be pity; and if pity is appropriate, *hamartia* cannot take the blame. Aristotle lands himself in inconsistency on the sole type of plot that he allows to be properly tragic. He is therefore left without any possible plot at all.

Fortunately the tragedians are not Aristotelians. They are able to use successfully three of his four types of plot. We have already noted instances of wholly virtuous heroes (or rather, heroines, a qualification not without interest). And it has often been pointed out that Shakespeare at least is able to use wicked men, like Macbeth and Richard III, as tragic heroes—so long as they exhibit, in Corneille's phrase, *grandeur d'âme. Greatness* of spirit; that is the essential quality of the tragic hero. Goodness, whether perfect or 'flawed', is not necessarily required, though it can certainly show itself to be a species of spiritual grandeur.

I have delayed too long over Aristotle, longer than his theory of Tragedy deserves. Little did he dream, poor man, that his scrappy remarks would be taken so seriously by later dramatists and critics. His fate at their hands is indeed unmerited, a fit object for our pity. It is the fashion among philosophers nowadays to praise Aristotle and belabour Aristotelians. Let us say, therefore, with a half measure of truth, that our over-long criticism is directed against the long line of his followers.

I do not intend to go through the theories of Tragedy proposed by later philosophers. There was a time when it would have been essential to discuss Hegel. But I think there is no need now to criticize Hegel's view of Tragedy, and unlike Aristotle he gets hisses from the fashionable first-nighters of the philosophical audience. The tale is

23

told (I have got it from Mr F. L. Lucas) that Hegel used to greet the Sunday joint with the words, 'Come, let us fulfil its destiny'. We may therefore leave him to his own Promethean destiny of being devoured when he is not left to grow cold on the shelf, and hope that he is able to acknowledge, with the Spartan resignation of his tragic hero, an eternal justice in his fate. Hegel did contribute something to the theory of Tragedy, as did Schopenhauer and Nietzsche. The trouble with all of them is that they approached their data with a ready-made metaphysics to which Tragedy had to be fitted willy-nilly.

The metaphysical problem from which they fashioned their Procrustean beds for Tragedy, is the problem of evil —by which I mean the existence of unmerited suffering. I have already allowed that a villain may be a tragic hero. Nevertheless, it seems to me, the poignancy of Tragedy comes out chiefly in the misery of innocence. All Tragedy deals with the presentation of evil, but some of the greatest works of tragic drama are concerned specifically with the metaphysical or theological problem of evil. If one already has some metaphysical theory of the world, some rational scheme into which all human experience is to be fitted, one approaches the problem of evil with an explanation ready made. The great tragedians do not inscribe evil under a prepared rubric. Sometimes they are groping their way to an explanation. Sometimes they seem to be denying that there is any explanation. Mostly, however, they are concerned simply to present the phenomenon of evil vividly before us, stamping it with a great question-mark and leaving us to answer the question as we can—if we can. Metaphysicians who already have their answer, be it optimistic like Hegel's or pessimistic like Schopenhauer's and Nietzsche's, distort the position of the tragic dramatist, whose first business is to express the disturbing character of the existence of evil, not to explain it or explain it away.

So far as I am aware, I have no ready-made solution to the problem of evil. I hope that the view of Tragedy which I shall put forward is derived from the evidence alone and not from a preconceived philosophy. I have little doubt, however, that preconceptions of *interest* have caused me to select certain aspects of tragic drama for emphasis, while a person whose main interests lay elsewhere would view Tragedy with a different focus. There is no single truth in philosophical generalization on matters of this kind. I shall be content if what I have to say succeeds in commending itself as *a* general truth about tragic drama.

Tragedy always presents a conflict. This proposition needs no defence. It is familiar enough. But a conflict between what? I suggest that it is a conflict between inevitable power, which we may call necessity, and the reaction to necessity of self-conscious effort. Tragic conflict differs from the conflicts presented by other forms of drama in that the victory always goes to necessity. The hero is crushed.

I have spoken of necessity, not fate. Writers on this subject often draw a distinction between classical Tragedy, which attributes human disaster to fate, and modern Tragedy, which attributes it to human character. For my purpose the distinction is irrelevant. In both cases, the cause of the disaster is necessity, whether external to the hero or inherent in his own character. For that matter, external necessity is not exhausted by fate or non-human powers. Antigone is in conflict with, and is crushed by, political power. (It is true that, in the same play, Creon opposes, and is in a different way struck down by, super-natural ordinance; but Antigone and her ordeal form the centre of interest.) In any event it is superficial to make the difference between classical and, say, Shakespearean Tragedy turn on a distinction between supernatural and psychological causes. Is Aeschylus' portrayal of Clytem-nestra in the *Agamemnon* a study of the workings of supernatural fate or of human psychology? It is either or both.[1] And the same is true of Shakespeare's treatment of Macbeth. You may choose, if you wish, to regard the workings of character as embodying dark forces that transcend the individual. Or you may regard myths, that speak of supernatural forces, as vivid expressions of the effects of psychological traits. *King Lear* is agreed to be the most nearly classical of Shakespeare's Tragedies; yet it can be treated as a study of pride and ingratitude. On the other side, is the psychological interest of Euripides' *Medea* any less than that of *Othello* or *Phèdre?*

The conflict, then, is with necessity, inevitable power that is bound to defeat any opposition. The tragic hero, even though he be a villain like Macbeth, attracts our admiration because of some *grandeur d'âme*, a greatness in his effort to resist, and our pity for his defeat. Although he must be crushed in his conflict, since his adversary is necessity, yet he does not yield the victory on all counts:

Capta ferum victorem cepit.

His *grandeur d'âme* is sublime and wins our admiration. Herein lies the satisfaction, the elevation, produced by Tragedy.

So far, I have not said anything particularly novel. Let

[1] Cf. Professor Kitto's account of the 'dual plane', discussed in §2 of the second essay in this book.

me now proceed to characterize further the aesthetic satisfaction of Tragedy. Tragic beauty is a species of the sublime. What is felt to be sublime is something surpassingly great.[1] It may be physically great or spiritually great, 'the starry heavens above' or 'the moral law within'. Both these, said Kant, fill us with wonder and awe. Now I want to suggest that the reaction to the sublime need not always be wonder *and awe*. It may be admiration alone. The works of God or Nature, 'the chains of the Pleiades, the bands of Orion'—when we feel these to be sublime, we feel wonder and awe. As A. C. Bradley says, our rapture goes along with self-surrender, with feelings of abasement no less than those of elevation. But what of the sublimity of human effort? When we see this, does our admiration include feelings of abasement? We may feel that we ordinary mortals could not rise to the heights of the tragic hero if we were in his place— though I shall try to show that the dramatist deliberately counters this by raising us in other ways above the characters in his play. At any rate, we do not feel that *man* is lowly, is dust and ashes, when confronted by the greatness of that which he opposes and by which he is crushed. He is defeated, but he remains great, sublime, in his fall. The greatness of his opponent is greatness of physical power. His own greatness is greatness of spirit. I suggest that at least some of the peculiar satisfaction of tragic drama comes from a feeling that the sublimity of the hero's spirit is superior to the sublimity of the power which overwhelms him. The dramatist stirs in us more admiration for the human spirit than awe for the powers of necessity.

Both Tragedy and Epic, as Aristotle says, elevate man

[1] Cf. A. C. Bradley, 'The Sublime', in *Oxford Lectures on Poetry*. London: Macmillan, 1909.

in their representation of human action, while Comedy abases him. Both Tragedy and Epic achieve the elevation of a hero through triumph in a conflict. Tragedy differs from Epic in that the tragic conflict and its issue are complicated and paradoxical. On the natural plane, the hero is worsted by the strength of his adversary, which thus appears great and, in the necessity of its conquest, sublime in the sense of awe-inspiring. On the spiritual plane, the hero appears great in his necessarily futile struggle. The inevitability of his defeat on the natural plane is what gives sublimity to his reaction. The inner conflict of Tragedy is between the two forms of the sublime, the awe-spiring strength of necessity and the *grandeur d'âme* which inspires admiration. Each triumphs on its own plane, but the triumph of the human spirit is the more elevating. And that is why the tragic fate of the hero gives us satisfaction.

Because Tragedy snatches a spiritual victory out of a natural defeat, it is nearer to the religious attitude than is Epic. In another way, however, Tragedy tends to be inimical to religion. It elevates man in his struggle with necessity, while the religious attitude is one of abasement before that which is greater than man, before the awe-inspiring sublime. This corollary of the sense of the tragic invites further discussion. Before pursuing it, we must return to pick up a thread left loose a short while ago.

The tragic hero, like the epic hero, Aristotle remarks, is given a nobility greater than that of life. As Anouilh says in his *Antigone*, futile reaction against necessity has no place in the life of ordinary men. 'It's a luxury (*C'est gratuit*). It's for kings.' Does it then follow that the audience of ordinary men feel themselves small before the grandeur of the superhuman heroes on the stage? No, it does not follow, for the dramatist employs his arts on the audience, too. He cannot give them superhuman nobility, such as he gives his hero, but in another way he raises them above his hero. A mark of the tragic hero is his limited knowledge, and the mark of tragic irony is the contrast between the hero's ignorance and the audience's knowledge, whereby statements that mean one thing to him have a *double entendre* for them. In his ignorance the tragic hero displays the finitude of man. The audience are free from this limitation. Within the universe of the play, they have the omniscience of the gods. A former colleague of mine, Mr D. H. Monro, in his book *Argument of Laughter*, speaks of the 'God's-eye view' of humanity presented in the Comedy of character. It is given in Tragedy, too. Indeed, in Greek Tragedy it is sometimes a view superior to that of a god. For if a god is brought upon the stage, the audience has a view embracing both the outlook of the god and that of the other characters. Even in *Prometheus Vinctus*, where Zeus never actually appears as a character on the stage, Aeschylus sets the audience above Zeus and Prometheus alike, for his aim is to seek a superior theology in which power and benevolence shall be combined, and in so far as he grasps and communicates such a 'God's-eye view' he places his audience at the vantage point from which that view may be obtained.

Tragedy is a form of art, and its pleasure is an aesthetic pleasure. We rarely, if ever, obtain from the so-called tragedies[1] of life the satisfaction that we gain from tragic

---

[1] It is important to bear in mind the distinction between tragic drama and 'tragedy' in a looser sense. I mark it by writing the word with a capital initial letter when it has the first meaning, and not when it has the second.

drama. In life, we are on the same level as those who suffer, we are fellow human beings. Our sympathy for their disaster is usually too strong for feelings of satisfaction at any sublimity they may display. In the theatre, the way is cleared for the appreciation of sublimity by giving us the 'God's-eye view'. The scene is set in the past, so that we know what is going to happen; or, if not in the past, in a distant clime, so that we shall not be too disposed to identify ourselves in sympathy with the characters on the stage. The dramatist fails in his purpose if, like Phrynichus with *The Capture of Miletus*, he represents life close to his audience and inhibits admiration by excessive pity.

Yet the separation must not go too far; for we shall be able to admire the human quality of the characters only if we feel sympathy for them as human beings ourselves. The author of Comedy, especially of satiric Comedy, can sometimes allow the distance between audience and stage to cross the boundary separating the human from the non-human. For instance, by dehumanizing his characters, as Karel Čapek does in *The Insect Play*, he completes the temporary deification of the audience—for he does not want them to sympathize. When the play is done, and they are brought back from divinity to humanity, they will see the beasts in themselves. The tragedian must raise his audience to the level of the God's-eye view, yet at the same time he must be careful not to deprive them of fellow-feeling with the characters on the stage.

He can succeed in this double purpose because the tragic hero is himself larger than life. The hero lacks the omniscience of his audience, but the gods who watch him, like the powers against whom he strives, fall below him in *grandeur d'âme*. Hero and adversary are balanced by their respective superiority in spiritual grandeur on the one side and natural power on the other. *Vis-à-vis* the audience, the spiritual grandeur of the hero is balanced by their godlike omniscience. Thus we can at the same time sympathize and admire. The hero is a man like us, showing human weaknesses from which the devices of art free us for the nonce; but though an object of our sympathy, he also seems sublime, for he outstrips us, and the superior powers whom he opposes, in greatness of spirit. And our sympathy for him as a fellow human being gives to his sublimity a stronger appeal than that exerted by the sublimity of the alien power with which he contends. By such devices Tragedy exalts man in our eyes. Its creed is humanistic.

The affinities of Tragedy with the sublime are emphasized by Mr Chu Kwang-Tsien in an interesting thesis whose scope is far wider than is indicated in its title, *The Psychology of Tragedy*.[1] He says (p. 11) that writers on aesthetics, with the possible exception of Burke, have 'never suspected' any close relation between the sense of the tragic and that of the sublime. This can hardly be true. A connection of some sort is too obvious to be overlooked, and perhaps writers on the subject have thought it too obvious to be mentioned. It may well be, however, that no one has previously explored the character of the connection, and this, as I hope my own suggestions have shown, is not so obvious or straightforward as one might suppose. Macneile Dixon uses the *word* 'sublime' at one or two points in his book on *Tragedy*, and no doubt others have done the same; but Macneile Dixon certainly does not develop any relation between Tragedy and the

[1] Strasbourg: Librairie Universitaire d'Alsace, 1933.

concept of the sublime. It is, I think, much to Mr Chu Kwang-Tsien's credit that he has done so, though I want to criticize the way in which he relates the two.

Chu Kwang-Tsien accepts the usual view that the sense of the sublime includes feelings of both admiration and awe, elevation and abasement. He suggests that the beauty of Tragedy is a species of the sublime, differing from other species in that the feelings which constitute the sense of the tragic include pity as well as admiration and awe. Putting his position in another way, he holds that Aristotle's addition of fear to Plato's pity is justified if one interprets fear as awe, and that wonder or admiration should probably be added, as suggested by Corneille, to Aristotle's two feelings of pity and fear.[1] Turning to the aesthetic descriptions of the objects of these states of mind, Chu Kwang-Tsien says that the object of aesthetic pity or sympathy is the graceful, which is usually tinged with a feeling of sadness; that the object of aesthetic admiration is grandeur, in the case of Tragedy heroic grandeur; and that the object of awe in Tragedy is the power of fate. (I find rather odd his linking of pity with the graceful, but I am not here concerned with the truth of that contention.) His general argument for including aesthetic fear or terror in the reaction to Tragedy, and therefore for classing the tragic with the sublime, runs as follows. Pity alone would give us the sense of sad gracefulness. This by itself is not tragic because not uplifting; it can be merely sentimental. We must add heroic grandeur, which arouses wonder and admiration. But if the heroic element predominates, the result will not be tragic; *Le Cid* is not tragic, while *Romeo and Juliet* is. To produce the sense of the tragic, the heroic element must be

[1] *The Psychology of Tragedy*, pp. 80–97.

balanced by 'the element of terror'. 'The merely terrible is in its effect just opposite to the heroic, each possesses what the other lacks. The heroic inspires us without first thrilling us with an emotion of fear, whereas the merely terrible thrills us with fear without inspiring us. The tragic must produce both effects at once.'[1] The fear which we feel in Tragedy is not, however, fear for the tragic hero or for ourselves, as Aristotle thought. 'In every case, it is the fear before the cruel and capricious visage of the Moirae, who have wrought all these "old, unhappy far-off things".'[2] This fear is followed by elevation. 'It calls forth an extraordinary amount of vital energy to cope with an extraordinary situation. It makes us equal to a tremendous task which in actual reality we can hardly hope to accomplish.' The pleasure of Tragedy is 'a pleasure that always accompanies overflowing life and intense activity'.[3]

It will be observed that Chu Kwang-Tsien's account has some features in common with mine but diverges from it in other respects. Where we differ, the thread of his argument seems to me to show certain weaknesses.

(1) He says that pity alone does not constitute the tragic emotion; there must be added admiration of heroic grandeur. With this I agree. He then says that heroic grandeur alone will not do, either, for the effect of heroic poetry or drama is not the same as that of Tragedy; and therefore he feels justified in adding an element of fear. But this second step in his argument seems to overlook the presence of pity. The tragic hero differs from the epic hero in being the object of pity as well as of admiration. There is

[1] *The Psychology of Tragedy*, p. 90.
[2] P. 95.
[3] P. 96.

no need to add fear in order to distinguish the tragic from the merely heroic.

(2) Chu Kwang-Tsien proceeds to vindicate the introduction of fear on the ground that the effect of Tragedy is that of the sublime, and the sublime always involves fear or abasement as well as admiration of grandeur. My own account has questioned this last proposition. May not an epic hero be sublime, even though he is not thwarted by fate? Chu Kwang-Tsien goes on to describe the fear of Tragedy as a feeling of awe before the power of fate, and he compares it with the fear and abasement before God of which Eliphaz speaks in the *Book of Job.* He would agree that the sense of the sublime in the *Book of Job,* and elsewhere, is a feeling both of wonder and of awe at surpassing grandeur and power found together, in God, or in any other being or thing that is sublime in this commonly acknowledged sense. The qualities exciting wonder and awe belong to the one object, and the two feelings are consequently directed upon the one object as sublime. Now when he previously argued that Tragedy must include grandeur to stir wonder and admiration, he referred to the grandeur of the tragic *hero. This* grandeur does not produce awe. Chu Kwang-Tsien himself says that the 'fear' or awe of Tragedy is not directed upon the individual hero but on fate. It follows that his analogy with the effect of the sublime, as he understands the sublime, is faulty. In his sense of the sublime, a sublime object is both great and terrible, and its greatness is what makes it terrible. But in characterizing Tragedy as a mode of the sublime, he has located the greatness in one place, in the tragic hero, and the cause of terror in another, in fate. Clearly he ought to have said that *fate,* as it appears in Tragedy, is sublime because both great

and terrible. What then will he say of the tragic hero? Is he or is he not sublime? If he is, we must admit that grandeur alone may be sublime. If he is not, then the requirement that Tragedy exhibit *heroic* grandeur is otiose. The combination of grandeur with the terrible or awe-inspiring is supplied by fate, and if that combination is all that is required for the sublimity of Tragedy, there is no need for grandeur in the characters.

(3) Finally, Chu Kwang-Tsien's account of tragic sublimity leaves him without any naturally ensuing explanation of the pleasure taken in Tragedy, and he has to resort to an *ad hoc* explanation which seems decidedly weak. He says that our fear of fate 'calls forth an extraordinary amount of energy to cope with an extraordinary situation'. The pleasure is 'a pleasure that always accompanies overflowing life and intense activity'. Well, the energy is called forth from the tragic hero more than from the audience. It is he, after all, not they, who has 'to cope with an extraordinary situation'. No doubt Chu Kwang-Tsien would say that we share the hero's energy by 'aesthetic sympathy' or empathy. Be it so. But it will be admitted that the energy communicated to us by the exercise of aesthetic imagination cannot be as great, or shall we say as real, as the energy which our imagination imitates. Then if the energy which we receive through imagination gives us pleasure, because pleasure 'always accompanies overflowing life and intense activity', it follows that the tragic hero must experience greater, or a more real, pleasure in his exercise of energy to cope with his extraordinary situation. Do the dramatists think so? Does Lear feel pleased as the blows of fate are doubled and redoubled upon him, requiring greater and greater effort to bear them? Is Macbeth enjoying himself when

he recognizes the force of necessity and faces it with words which undoubtedly give *us* enjoyment of the sublime?

> Tomorrow, and tomorrow, and tomorrow,
> Creeps in this petty pace from day to day,
> Until the last syllable of recorded time;
> And all our yesterdays have lighted fools
> The way to dusty death.

Chu Kwang-Tsien finds the distinction between the sublimity of Tragedy and other forms of sublimity purely in the fact that the tragic emotion includes pity. I have suggested that the peculiar mark of tragic sublimity is that Tragedy presents a conflict between two forms of the sublime and makes one of these, the sublimity of human heroism, appeal to us more than the other. I agree that tragic sympathy is important here, but I have tried to show how it is. Sympathy with the tragic hero causes us to appreciate his sublimity more warmly than that of the power which confronts him. Our pleasure arises from the feeling that one like us reaches the greater height. In my view, therefore, abasement has no place in the tragic emotion. This leads me at once to say something more about the relation between tragic drama and religion.

2

Tragedy and Religion

IT HAS often been noted that Tragedy faces the problems
that lie at the heart of religion. Although Tragedy does
not have a directly moral purpose, as Aristotle and Hegel
suppose, it is deeply concerned with morality. It deals
with evil and the effects of evil. Above all, the great
tragedians are disturbed by injustice, and are led to
wonder whether the power that moves the world is just.
Not all Tragedy, not even all great Tragedy, is occupied
with this particular problem, but it certainly appears in
many of the greatest tragic dramas.

Thus Tragedy comes near to religion. But there are
two reasons why the path of Tragedy tends to diverge
from that of religion as we understand it in our Biblical
tradition. First, Judaism and Christianity take it for granted
that God must be just, and that the problem of innocent
suffering must have a solution. If a tragedian insists upon
such a solution (as Aeschylus seems to do), his approach to
the problem is compatible with the religious spirit. But if,
as more often happens, he simply pinpoints the problem
without offering any solution, his attitude is not that of religious faith but of the religious questioning that leaves open
the gate to scepticism at least as wide as the gate to faith.

The issue is stated concisely and categorically by Professor I. A. Richards:

'Tragedy is only possible to a mind which is for the moment agnostic or Manichean. The least touch of any theology which has a compensating Heaven to offer the tragic hero is fatal.'[1]

Less satisfactorily, Professor Karl Jaspers confines himself to the destiny of the hero and omits the implication for theology proper:

'Christian salvation opposes tragic knowledge. The chance of being saved destroys the tragic sense of being trapped without chance of escape. Therefore no genuinely Christian tragedy can exist.'[2]

Both these writers affirm their universal propositions with a confidence equalled only by their brevity. Evidently they think it unnecessary to discuss any apparently negative instances. For Professor Richards there is no need, since he considers that only a bare handful of so-called Tragedies deserve the name anyway. He admits the six masterpieces of Shakespeare. Practically all the rest of tragic drama, including the whole of Greek Tragedy, he regards as 'pseudo-tragedy'. Professor Jaspers is more liberal—but less clear about his position. Earlier in his book he has listed different types of tragic drama, among them the 'Christian Tragedy' of Racine and Calderón; but when he decides that 'no genuinely Christian tragedy can exist', he does not say anything clearly to indicate whether he thinks the plays of Racine and Calderón fail to be tragic or fail to be Christian.

A more careful statement of the position of Tragedy in

[1] *Principles of Literary Criticism*, London: Kegan Paul, 1924, p. 246.
[2] *Tragedy Is Not Enough*, London: Gollancz, 1953, p. 38.

relation to religion is given by the late Professor Una Ellis-Fermor:

'The tragic mood is balanced between the religious and the non-religious interpretations of catastrophe and pain, and the form, content, and mood of the play which we call a tragedy depend upon a kind of equilibrium maintained by these opposite readings of life, to neither of which the dramatist can wholly commit himself.'[1]

This does not differ radically from I. A. Richards's statement that the tragic mood is 'agnostic or Manichean'. Indeed there is one place[2] where Miss Ellis-Fermor definitely espouses the second alternative, speaking of 'that Manichaeistic balance from which tragedy springs'. She also repeats Richards's point about 'a compensating Heaven' when she says that 'progression into beatitude' makes Tragedy impossible.[3] The value of her contribution lies in her insistence that the 'balance' or 'equilibrium' of the tragic attitude lies between a religious and a non-religious impression of suffering. She explains the difference in this way. The non-religious impression is simply an 'intense awareness of evil and pain'. The religious is an inkling of 'some reconciliation with or interpretation in terms of good'. If there is a conflict in the mind between the two impressions, there arises 'a sense of mystery', an 'assumption that evil can never be sounded, . . . that its causes will never fully reveal themselves, even to the most passionate questioning'.[4]

Another variation on the same theme can be found in

[1] *The Frontiers of Drama*, London: Methuen, 1945, pp. 17–18.
[2] P. 146.
[3] P. 23n.
[4] P. 128.

the book of Mr Chu Kwang-Tsien to which I referred in the preceding section. He not only illustrates from the Bible and from the drama of Christian Europe the thesis that Tragedy and religion do not mix, but also considers the evidence from China and India, where, he tells us, the drama has not included Tragedy. A. W. Schlegel, in his comparison (published in 1807) between Racine's *Phèdre* and Euripides' *Hippolytus*, pointed out the discrepancy between the Greek idea of tragic fatality and the Christian idea of Providence, and suggested that a Christian poet might find it impossible to compose a genuine Tragedy. Chu Kwang-Tsien turns Schlegel's 'might' into a 'must'.

'With its emphasis on the moral order of the world, on Original Sin and Last Judgment, on submission and humility, Christianity is in every sense antagonistic to the spirit of Tragedy. Tragedy, as it represents the struggle of man with Fate, and as it often expresses vividly to our eyes inexplicable evils and undeserved sufferings, has always something profane and blasphemous in it.'[1]

Elsewhere, he goes farther and insists that Tragedy is hostile not only to Christianity but to religion in general and to all metaphysics. (I should explain that he restricts the name of 'religion' to those faiths which include a *consistent* theology, and he therefore denies that the Greek ideas of the gods constituted a religion.) Both religion and metaphysical philosophy, he says, think they can solve the problem of evil by means of some dogma. The dogma quiets our questioning and satisfies the intellect or at least the emotions. Tragedy, however, finds no solution to the problem of evil. It, too, gives repose and satisfaction,

[1] *The Psychology of Tragedy*, p. 236.

but in a different way, simply by presenting 'brilliant images' of the suffering that poses the problem. It 'suspends judgment and loses itself in aesthetic contemplation'.[1] At the same time, Chu Kwang-Tsien notes that 'religion is born of the sense of the tragic'.[2] From the pessimism and puzzlement of the tragic attitude, one may come to accept religious hope for the future. But when that has been done, the sense of the tragic is lost or diminished.

The four writers whose views I have mentioned constitute a fair sample of weighty opinion to the effect that Tragedy is incompatible with religion. There is weighty opinion on the other side, too; and there is room for it, if the case against religious Tragedy is confined to the single main point that comes out of the remarks I have quoted. All these remarks turn upon the way in which one faces the problem of evil, of undeserved suffering. I have already agreed that this problem forms the centre of interest in many of the greatest Tragedies. But it is not so in all, and if the antagonism between Tragedy and optimistic religion rests upon their respective attitudes to innocent suffering, we shall have to say that such a religion makes impossible not all, but certain types of, tragic drama.

There is, however, a second reason why religion, as understood in our Biblical tradition, tends to be inimical to Tragedy. This second reason follows from the answer I have given to the question why Tragedy pleases. According to my suggestion, our pleasure is the result of regarding the tragic hero as more sublime than the power he opposes. Now if this power be identified, as it often is,

[1] *The Psychology of Tragedy*, p. 213.
[2] P. 215.

41

with the supreme power that moves the world, the spiritual grandeur of a human being is exalted above the omnipotence of nature or 'fate'. A theology which makes the power of nature an expression of the power of God, must regard such a situation in Tragedy as exalting human worth above the omnipotence of God. I think that Biblical religion would find this, rather than perplexity at innocent suffering, the 'something profane and blasphemous' in Tragedy. Not all tragic heroes are struggling against the power of 'fate' or nature. Where they do so, whether natural power be represented as fate or psychological necessity, Biblical religion must look askance at the exaltation of human defiance. The second ground of opposition supplements the first. Neither alone applies to all Tragedy. But between the two of them it will not be easy to find a type of Tragedy which can avoid religious offence.

There is an implicit reference to the second reason in Chu Kwang-Tsien's mention of 'submission and humility' among the characteristics of Christianity that are antagonistic to Tragedy, but in his development of the general theme he does not follow up this point. One aspect of it was noted long ago by the seventeenth-century critic Saint-Évremond, when discussing Corneille's dramatization of the martyrdom of Polyeucte:

'The spirit of our Religion is diametrically opposed to that of Tragedy. The humility and patience of our Saints are too much the contrary of the virtues which the Theatre demands of Heroes.'[1]

---

[1] *De la Tragédie ancienne et moderne* (1672). I take the original of my quotation, and likewise the references to Dacier (*Poétique d'Aristote*) and Lessing (*Hamburgische Dramaturgie*), from J. G. Robertson, *Lessing's Dramatic Theory*, Cambridge University Press, 1939, pp. 421–3.

He goes on to say that Corneille's Polyeucte shows excessive zeal and ardour for a Christian. In the subsequent continuation, by other critics, of discussion of *Polyeucte* and of martyrdom as a possible subject of tragic drama, the red herring of Aristotelian doctrine obscured the issue. Dacier thinks the trouble is simply that Polyeucte is 'a highly virtuous man' and therefore cannot be a tragic hero; for, in accordance with Aristotle's dictum about unqualified virtue, he cannot arouse pity and fear so as to purge the passions. Likewise Lessing says that a Christian hero is unsuited to the tragic purpose of *catharsis*. This, of course, simply misses the point. Saint-Évremond came near to it when he saw that the *kind* of virtue which is admired in a tragic hero tends to be the opposite of humility, or at least of humble submission.

I have given two reasons for finding it difficult to accommodate Tragedy to Biblical religion. In order to understand clearly why they are obstacles, we need to consider them against the background of Biblical *theology*. The first difficulty is that of reconciling divine justice with the undeserved suffering we find in the world. I. A. Richards is obviously right in implying that the tragic treatment of evil is compatible with Manichaeism. It is, however, liable to conflict with orthodox Monotheism, in which absolute goodness and justice are combined with absolute power in one God. The second difficulty is that of reconciling our religious beliefs with the quality of our admiration for the tragic hero. A tragic hero may display *some* of the typically Biblical virtues—righteousness, love, and patience. But humility is not easily made heroic; and if the tragic hero strives against omnipotence, admiration of his heroism is impious for a theology which unites omnipotence with absolute goodness. Let me illustrate the difference that Biblical theology makes.

In *Prometheus Vinctus*, Aeschylus stages a conflict between divine power and divine benevolence to mankind. Zeus represents the one, Prometheus the other. Aeschylus suggests that Zeus' imperfection arises because he is a young god; he has not yet had time to learn. His power is not backed by the wisdom that would enable him to wield power justly. Plainly, Aeschylus is himself *developing* a religion in which supreme power may be united with supreme wisdom and goodness. Until this will be accomplished, there is tragic conflict between the power of heaven and the relative impotence of wisdom (foresight, *prometheia*) that seeks to do good. The *Oresteia* discloses a similar development of thought. Older ideas of justice lead to unending evil and conflict; and Aeschylus gropes his way to the conception of a divine justice that will result in unmixed good. The old gods are to be reconciled with the new. In the *Agamemnon* and the *Choëphoroe* we are presented with the tragic conflict. The *Eumenides* resolves the conflict and puts an end to the tragic situation.

The theology of the Hebrews reached at a very early stage the idea of a single, all-embracing God, in whom omnipotence, omniscience, justice, and goodness are bound together in unity. It follows from such a theology that there can be no conflict between the effects of these attributes in the world. There cannot be any undeserved evil, or any discrepancy between the power of natural law and the fruits of virtue. Accordingly, there is no tragedy in the Bible. This is not to say that there is no innocent suffering. For instance, Abel and Jephthah's daughter are both innocent victims of an untimely death. But the stories of their death, as told in the Bible, are not allowed to raise any theological problem. The evil is caused by man, and the moral is that we can and should choose to avoid the sins of Cain and Jephthah. Human freedom is real and effective. It can cause evil, to ourselves and others. Equally it can realize good. The choice is ours. Of course, the theological problem still lies there for those who wish to uncover it. Why should the sins of Cain and Jephthah be allowed to bring evil to the innocent as well as to themselves? But the Biblical writers do not face this problem until we come to such books as *Job*, the *Psalms*, and *Isaiah*. In the earlier narrative of the Bible there is plenty of *material* for Tragedy. Chu Kwang-Tsien points out the similarity between the story of Jephthah's daughter and that of Iphigeneia; and Milton tried to make a Tragedy out of the story of Samson. As told in the Bible, however, these stories are not presented as tragedy but as moral lessons on the dire effects of human guilt, and if the events described are moral lessons they serve a good purpose. It is presumed that all will work out for the best in the end. There is no sense of *wasted* goodness, which, as A. C. Bradley says,[1] is essential to Tragedy.

Even when the Psalmist is driven by the experience of life to protest at the injustice of innocence cast down and wickedness exalted, he does not doubt that all will come right in the end. His regret, always temporary, is simply that God's fulfilment of justice seems over-long to the impatient human heart. Yet though the Psalmist's hope be realized eventually, when the righteous prosper and the wicked be punished, there remains the problem that the interim suffering of the righteous is unmerited. This problem is faced in *Isaiah*, Chapters XLIX–LIII, and in

[1] *Shakespearean Tragedy*, London: Macmillan, 1904, p. 37.

the *Book of Job*. The *Book of Job* does not give us an answer; it bids us cease our questioning. *Isaiah* gives an answer without first raising any questioning doubts. In both there is complete faith in God, but the *Book of Job* in raising the question comes nearer to the spirit of the Greek tragedians, while *Isaiah* reaches the greater depth of religious insight or speculation.

The doctrine of 'the suffering servant' is, I suppose, the most profound solution offered by religion to the problem of evil. The innocent servant of God suffers for the sins of others, to the end that they may be brought to see their own unworthiness and guilt. And what of justice? Innocent suffering for the good of others is unjust only if it be *imposed* from outside. If the innocent sufferer has himself *chosen* to be the instrument of good, no question of justice arises. *Isaiah*, Chapter LIII, seems to include both ideas:

Yet *it pleased the Lord* to crush him by disease;
To see if his soul *would offer itself* in restitution, . . .
And that *the purpose of the Lord* might prosper by his hand.[1]

The doctrine of Isaiah appears to include the view of the *Book of Job* that God imposes suffering on the innocent in order to test and enhance their goodness, and at the same time it goes farther in making their voluntary submission a means, chosen by God and his servant jointly, for bringing about improvement in others. The suffering is imposed by God, but the servant voluntarily accepts it and takes it upon himself as atonement for the wicked.

[1] LIII, 10. The italics are, of course, mine. In quoting from the Old Testament, I use the version of *The Holy Scriptures* issued by the Jewish Publication Society of America (Philadelphia: 1917).

And the Lord hath made to light on him
The iniquity of us all.
He was oppressed, though he humbled himself
And opened not his mouth. . . .
Yet he bore the sin of many,
And made intercession for the transgressors.[1]

Earlier chapters of *Isaiah* take the traditional view that suffering must be punishment for one's own sins. This is to deny that there is any innocent suffering. In the section on 'the suffering servant', the prophet acknowledges its existence. Yet it is never allowed to be a *problem*, to raise questions and doubts. As soon as the existence of unmerited evil is recognized, the religious spirit finds in it a heightened goodness and a means to good. The moral order of the universe is not dimmed, but shines with a more brilliant light than before.

The *Book of Job* is different. Here, for once, the problem of evil raises doubt, and no solution is provided. *Job* has been likened to a Greek Tragedy, and especially to *Prometheus Vinctus* both in form and in subject-matter. Certainly it comes nearer to Tragedy than anything else in the Bible. Yet it is not a Tragedy. The effect intended and produced on the reader is quite different.

The mere fact that Job is restored to prosperity in the epilogue does not matter very much, irrespective of whether we regard this as a later addition or not. After all, the epilogue itself acknowledges that evil done cannot be undone, for it says that Job's relations and friends 'bemoaned him, and comforted him concerning all the evil that the Lord had brought upon him',[2] and this even after God had given him twice what he had before. The

[1] LIII, 6–7, 12.
[2] XLII, 11.

Book of Job is not a Tragedy, because the grandeur of the hero is deliberately shrunk to nothing before the sublimity of the power he has questioned. Compare Chapter XIII, verses 15–16, with Chapter XLII, verse 6:

> Behold, He will slay me; I wait for Him: [or: I have no hope:][1]
> But I will argue my ways before Him.
> This also shall be my salvation,
> That a hypocrite cannot come before Him.

[1] For the alternative renderings here, cf. the margin of the Revised Version. The American Jewish version follows the inspired rendering of the Authorized Version: 'Though he slay me, yet will I trust in him'.

'I have no hope' translates the reading of the Hebrew text, which literally means 'I do not wait (for anything better)'. It is traditional to follow the Massoretic reading in the margin, which substitutes for the Hebrew word *lo*, meaning 'not', a similarly sounded but differently spelt word meaning 'to or for him'. (Confusion between these two words occurs several times in the text of the Hebrew Bible.) This gives the meaning, 'I wait for him'; and since the verb used seems always to connote waiting *hopefully* and never waiting for anything evil (cf. the philological note on the passage by S. R. Driver and G. B. Gray, *International Critical Commentary* on the *Book of Job*, Edinburgh: T. & T. Clark, 1921, Pt. II, pp. 84–5), there is perhaps some justification for the idea behind the A.V. rendering, 'yet will I trust in him', though it cannot be strictly correct.

The reading in the Hebrew text is more what we might expect, and more in the spirit of a tragic hero. But the marginal reading is supported by most of the non-Hebrew ancient versions. In any case, even if the original story, which was not Hebraic, made Job say 'I have no hope', the traditional reading expresses the way in which Judaism insisted on adapting it. It is typical of the Old Testament to adapt to the spirit of its own religion material originally gathered from an external source (cf. the Biblical treatment of the story of the Flood); and it is that spirit—not the spirit of its pre-Biblical material —which I am here contrasting with the spirit of Tragedy.

I am indebted to Dr David Daiches for pointing out to me that the traditional translation, 'Though he slay me, yet will I trust in him', depends on a marginal reading, and that the text gives quite a different sense.

Here Job is sublime, equally matched in debate with God. But in the end, when God has reminded him of the limitations of human understanding, he says:

> Wherefore I abhor my words, and repent,
> Seeing I am dust and ashes.

One might perhaps say that Job is still sublime if one felt that so bold a spirit could not acknowledge his nonentity without great effort. Still, the main point is that the result of Job's contest with God shows God superior in every way. Job has demonstrated the truth of God's description of him to Satan:

> Hast thou considered My servant Job, that there is none like him in the earth, a whole-hearted and upright man, one that feareth God, and shunneth evil? and he still holdeth fast his integrity, although thou didst move Me against him, to destroy him without cause.[1]

If we think of a contest between Job and Satan, Job is spiritually victorious. But that is not where the interest of the book lies. Job's conflict is in debate with God, and at the end he humbly concedes God's superiority in the debate as well as in power.

Observe, too, that when Job does contend with God, he opposes only his *understanding* to God's justice. There is never any question of opposing his will, of refusing to *accept* the order of the world. He questions its justice but he submits to it willingly. In the very place where Job is most bold, in declaring that he will argue his ways before God, he also acknowledges, with humble acceptance, God's power: 'Behold, He will slay me; I wait for Him' (or: 'I have no hope'). Job joins the questioning intellect of a

[1] II, 3.

49

Greek with the submissive faith of a Hebrew. The verse matches man with God, in the manner of Greek Tragedy, but at the same time it matches intellectual audacity with submission of the will.[1] In the end, however, Job abases his intellect to an equal depth of submission: 'I abhor my words, and repent, seeing I am dust and ashes'.

We cannot say that the problem of evil is ignored in the *Book of Job*, nor that it is solved. No solution is given for the intellectual difficulty. We are told that it is a mystery too great for the human understanding to penetrate. The difference between *Job* and Tragedy, therefore, does not lie in different approaches to the problem of evil. Many writers on Tragedy stress the sense of mystery that lurks in the wings of the tragic drama. Tragedy, they tell us, does not try to solve the problem of evil; it merely presents the problem, and leaves it as a mystery. So does the *Book of Job*. Accordingly we cannot say that Biblical religion, unlike Tragedy, *always* assumes that the problem of evil can be solved. For that matter, not all Tragedy leaves the problem as a mystery. Aeschylus seeks a solution in feeling his way to a theology of the kind presupposed in our Bible. Euripides on the other hand tends to seek a solution in a rejection of the gods. Neither is prepared merely to leave the problem as a mystery.

When we turn, however, to the other cause of strain between Tragedy and Biblical religion, their respective attitudes to kicking against the pricks, we find that this is illustrated most forcibly in the *Book of Job*. Job is commended in the epilogue for having spoken of God 'the thing that is right', unlike his comforters. He is com-

---

[1] If we could accept the A.V. rendering, 'Though he slay me, yet will I trust in him', the contrast between this absolute degree of faith and the accompanying audacity would be itself sublime.

mended, and they are rebuked, for what is said about the conventional view that all suffering is punishment for sin. But Job is himself rebuked for daring to argue with God:

> Shall he that reproveth contend with the Almighty?
> He that argueth with God, let him answer it.

And Job answers:

> Behold, I am of small account; what shall I answer Thee?
> I lay my hand upon my mouth.[1]

Tragedy glorifies human resistance to necessity, religion praises submission. To put it crudely with Anouilh, the tragic hero says 'No' to the forces which oppose and crush him; religion commends resignation. Iphigeneia tries to escape her fate; Jephthah's daughter accepts hers without question. Prometheus defies Zeus; Job lays his hand upon his mouth.

To sum up, the religion of the Bible is inimical to Tragedy, first because it is optimistic and trusts that evil is always a necessary means to greater good, and secondly because it abases man before the sublimity of God. Tragedy on the other hand treats evil as unalloyed evil; it regrets the waste of human worth of any kind, and does not think that innocent suffering can be justified. Secondly, it shows human effort to be sublime, a fit match for the sublimity of nature and nature's gods. If this is true, it will follow that Tragedy is hardly possible against a background of Biblical religion. Is that conclusion borne out by the history of the drama in Christian Europe?

In the Middle Ages, so far as I know, there is no tragic drama. It is, I think, quite implausible to suggest that

[1] XL, 2, 4.

Shakespeare's Tragedies rest on Christian theology. Those who try to make out that Shakespeare's Tragedies are Christian, tend to forget just how much is involved in Christian belief. To illustrate the point, I shall discuss an attempt to interpret *King Lear* as an expression of Christian doctrine. More promising suggestions of negative instances to the general thesis that Tragedy and religion do not mix, are to be found in Milton, Corneille, and Racine. I gather that Calderón also wrote what is called Christian Tragedy, but I know nothing of his work or of Spanish, so I must hope that the examples I shall deal with will be sufficiently instructive.

Most people would say, I think, that *King Lear* obviously supports my generalization. It has been called the most fatalistic, the most Aeschylean, and the most heathen, of Shakespeare's Tragedies. Edgar and Albany give expression to orthodox sentiments of divine justice, but these sound trite and superficial against Gloucester's lines:

> As flies to wanton boys, are we to the gods;
> They kill us for their sport.

It has been suggested, however, by Professor J. F. Danby,[1] that *King Lear* is a study in the orthodox teaching on Christian patience:

'Cordelia is the perfection of Christian patience that suffereth long and is kind. Her father is an instance of extreme falling off—first into rage and then into madness. Gloucester and Edgar occupy a middle region between these two limits. The son is sturdily patient. The father

[1] '*King Lear* and Christian Patience', in *The Cambridge Journal*, Vol. I (1947–8), pp. 305 ff.

wavers on the edge of grace and despair and is only saved in the end by the ministrations of his son.'[1]

For my purpose, it does not matter whether Shakespeare's representation of the virtue of patience in *King Lear* is Christian or Stoic. Professor Danby's case may be allowed so far as ethics is concerned. But when people ask whether the 'philosophy' of *King Lear* (or of Shakespeare's Tragedies in general) is Christian or pagan, they are thinking of theology as much as ethics. In considering the theology, it is of little importance that the characters of *King Lear* speak, except in one place, of 'gods' in the plural rather than of 'God' in the singular. The point is whether the ways of God or the gods are justified or not. Cordelia may display the perfection of Christian patience, but unless her fate is shown not to be a waste of goodness, Shakespeare's treatment of it is not Christian.

By 'the perfection of Christian patience' is meant an imitation of the patience of Jesus. Now the story of Jesus, as told in the Christian Gospels, is not tragic, precisely because of the supernatural interpretation of the purpose of his passion. Imagine a pagan hearing the history of Jesus, and dismissing as superstition both the supernatural interpretation of it and the report of a miraculous resurrection. If such a pagan were a dramatic artist, he could make of the story a Tragedy of the highest order. The hero shows great human qualities, inspires high hopes in his followers, comes into conflict with the powers that be, and perishes with a cry of despair, 'My God, my God, why has thou forsaken me?' Add the Christian doctrine of the divinity of Jesus, and of the redemption secured by his passion; at once the situation ceases to be

[1] Danby, p. 314.

tragic. The virtue and death of Cordelia are presented in *King Lear* as the story of Jesus might be presented by my hypothetical pagan dramatist.

Even if we confine ourselves to the grandeur of human quality in the face of adversity, we must admit that the perfection of patience is not shown, in *King Lear*, as the sum and crown of such grandeur. *Morally*, Lear is a less admirable character than Cordelia, but Shakespeare makes him the main tragic hero of the play, and wins for him our strongest expression of the tragic emotions of pity and admiration. Professor Danby quotes, among other references to patience, the line (in Act II, scene iv):

> You heavens, give me that patience, patience I need!

Lear is trying to control himself in the face of Goneril's and Regan's argument that he has no need of followers. As I read his speech, he is trying to control a breakdown into tears, a failure of will. He says:

> But for true need,—
> You heavens, give me that patience, patience I need!
> You see me here, you gods, a poor old man,
> As full of grief as age; wretched in both!
> If it be you that stir these daughters' hearts
> Against their father, fool me not so much
> To bear it tamely; touch me with noble anger,
> And let not woman's weapons, water-drops,
> Stain my man's cheeks!

Mr Danby interprets this as an effort to retain patience followed immediately by failure to do so:

'Even after the admission of his true need he calls on the gods to fool him not so much "to bear it tamely". He would have "noble anger" and inexpressible revenge.'[1]

[1] Danby, p. 315.

I cannot myself find a *reversal* of pleas to the gods in Lear's speech here. However that may be, Lear's grandeur as a tragic figure depends on the fact that he does not 'bear tamely' his adversities but shows 'noble anger' against daughters and gods alike.

There is no doubt that throughout the play Shakespeare recalls traditional Christian doctrine. But it can hardly be said that he is subscribing to it. Both Lear and Gloucester are taught by their suffering to feel compassion for the lowly, a compassion they could not feel in their former success. Lear learns his lesson on the heath (Act III, scene iv). He prays for 'poor naked wretches', and ends:

> Take physic, pomp;
> Expose thyself to feel what wretches feel,
> That thou mayest shake the superflux to them,
> And show the heavens more just.

'Show the heavens more just.' At once Shakespeare makes 'the heavens' give another turn to the screw; Edgar utters the first words of his pretended madness, and Lear goes genuinely mad. Edgar is the man who believes 'the gods are just'. Shakespeare's irony makes this orthodox believer, in feigned madness, bring real madness to Lear just at the point when Lear has been converted, by the orthodox method, to the orthodox belief. 'Show the heavens more just' indeed. They will show you now how just.

A. C. Bradley, in his *Shakespearean Tragedy*,[1] thinks that the deaths of Cordelia and Lear at the end of the play are not dramatically justified. The tragic emotions, he says, have been stirred enough, and he would like to give Lear 'peace and happiness by Cordelia's fireside', the

[1] Pp. 252–4.

humble happiness of which Lear speaks when he says:

> Come, let's away to prison:
> We two alone will sing like birds i' the cage:
> When thou dost ask me blessing, I'll kneel down,
> And ask of thee forgiveness: so we'll live,
> And pray, and sing, and tell old tales, and laugh
> At gilded butterflies, . . .

Bradley ends his quotation at this point. But let us go on a little:

> and hear poor rogues
> Talk of court news; and we'll talk with them too,—
> Who loses and who wins; who's in, who's out;—
> And take upon's the mystery of things,
> As if we were God's spies:

There: can one imagine Lear turning himself into one of 'God's spies', who profess knowledge of the ways of divine justice in the ups and downs of life? This is the one place in the play where Shakespeare speaks of 'God' in the singular. It is hardly a recommendation of orthodoxy. Bradley himself calls it a 'scornful rebuke' when, at a later stage of his discussion, he says that Edgar's and Albany's belief in divine justice is not the view of Shakespeare:

'Is not his mind rather expressed in the bitter contrast between their faith and the events we witness, or in the scornful rebuke of those who take upon them the mystery of things as if they were God's spies?'[1]

I think this answers sufficiently both Bradley's earlier suggestion that Lear should have been left to live out the life of a bird in the cage, and anyone else's suggestion that the play is conformable to Christian doctrine.

[1] *Shakespearean Tragedy*, p. 274.

I have not been arguing that the mood of *King Lear* is one of total pessimism. I should agree that this play, like the other Tragedies of Shakespeare, illustrates Bradley's general thesis[1] that the order of the tragic universe 'shows itself akin to good and alien from evil'. The main source of tragic calamity, he continues, is evil, which is cast out by the order of the world. Such an order 'cannot be friendly to evil or indifferent between evil and good'. But this is not enough to make it the order of the world postulated by Biblical theology. As Bradley says, the tragic process, in casting out evil, is forced to *waste good*. Any *waste* of good must be impossible in the universe of Biblical religion, where God is omnipotent as well as perfectly good.

More plausible examples of religious Tragedy are provided by Milton's *Samson Agonistes* and Corneille's *Polyeucte*. The latter was expressly sub-entitled '*Tragédie Chrétienne*', and occasioned controversy among Corneille's contemporaries on the question whether a religious theme could or should be displayed in the theatre. The *dramatic* success of the play is not now in question; nor do I wish to deny the *poetic* qualities of either *Polyeucte* or *Samson Agonistes*. But I shall perhaps not be alone in reporting that a reading of these two pieces does not give rise to the specific aesthetic feelings occasioned by Tragedy. When I try to analyse the reasons for this, they turn out to be much the same for both works. In neither is the hero an object of pity; his death is not presented as a sheer waste of human quality, but is a means to good, so that the reversal of fortune brought about by the poet is from lesser to greater good, or from greater to lesser evil.

[1] *Shakespearean Tragedy*, pp. 33 ff.

At the beginning of Milton's poem, Samson and the Hebrews are already in the depths of shame and despair, while the Philistines triumph. At the end, the Philistines are destroyed and the Hebrews thus saved from their enemies. On the supernatural level, the Philistine god Dagon has been shown false and impotent, while the God of the Hebrews has exerted miraculous power and executed justice. Where is the tragedy? Samson has died. But he has chosen his death willingly and gladly; it is the means of executing divine justice on the Philistines; and it is, both for Samson and for his people, less evil than his shameful captivity. Samson himself has expressed the wish for death all along. The *peripeteia* ('reversal of fortune') consists in the fact that the expected evil of his death, though it remains a death, turns unexpectedly into a good—both on the material plane, for the well-being of his people, and on the spiritual plane, for the reputation of Samson and Samson's God. The victory goes on all counts to the side with whom we are expected to sympathize. The only person on that side who has his hopes dashed down by Samson's death is Manoa. But he soon recognizes that the disappointment of his expectation of ransom and release is no subject for pity:

> Come, come, no time for lamentation now,
> Nor much more cause, Samson hath quit himself
> Like Samson, and heroicly hath finish'd
> A life Heroic, on his Enemies
> Fully reveng'd, . . .
> > To Israel
> Honour hath left, and freedom, . . .
> To himself and Fathers house eternal fame;
> And which is best and happiest yet, all this
> With God not parted from him, as was feard,
> But favouring and assisting to the end.

Nothing is here for tears, nothing to wail
Or knock the breast, no weakness, no contempt,
Dispraise, or blame, nothing but well and fair,
And what may quiet us in a death so noble.

The death of a hero does not make a Tragedy, even when, as in *Samson Agonistes*, there is no expectation of any life beyond death. Still less so when death leads to the beatitude of heaven, as in Corneille's *Polyeucte*. Polyeucte is an Armenian of the Roman Empire, who, at the beginning of the play, becomes a Christian and at once desires to seek martyrdom by breaking the idols of the dominant religion. He breaks the idols, and then has some difficulty in getting himself martyred; for the Governor of the province, Félix, is his father-in-law, and both Félix and his daughter Pauline try to persuade Polyeucte to recant and save his life. Polyeucte is thus involved in the sham Cornelian conflict between duty and love, sham because duty always wins. So Polyeucte has his way and is duly martyred. When told that he is going 'to death', he replies 'To glory'. All along he has sought death. In Act II, his fellow-Christian, Néarque, tries to dissuade him from a rash iconoclasm. Néarque tells him, 'You will find death'; and Polyeucte replies, 'I seek it for the sake of God'. When Néarque urges him to live, in order to protect, with his high status, the Christians of the province, Polyeucte says that the example of his death will strengthen them more. Neither Polyeucte nor the audience finds anything to regret in his death. It causes both his wife and his father-in-law to become Christians, and it confirms the resolve of the pagan Sévère to protect Christians whenever he can. As in *Samson Agonistes*, all turns out for the best; the hero seeks his death and effects good by it.

Most of the characters are involved in the typical Cor-

nelian conflict, and it is always a foregone conclusion that
they will follow duty instead of passion. Corneille thinks
this is the height of sublimity. Pauline was in love with
Sévère, but has married Polyeucte out of deference to her
father's wishes, and Sévère himself is made to say:

> *Je nommais inconstance, et prenais pour un crime*
> *De ce juste devoir l'effort le plus sublime.*

It comes so often, this overt appeal to duty, that one cannot help regarding both Polyeucte and Pauline as prigs.
One sees the point of Mr F. L. Lucas's remark, 'The objection to perfect characters is not that their misfortunes are,
as Aristotle says, unbearable, but that they are apt themselves to be so'.[1] The only character in *Polyeucte* that
wins any real sympathy from us is Sévère, who has to give
up his love without the compensation of Christian com-
fort which leaves the converts, Polyeucte, Pauline, and
Félix, so happy. If there is any tragic hero at all in the
play, it is Sévère. One feels as much admiration for him
as for Pauline, and more than for Polyeucte. Like
Sévère, Pauline could be the object of our sympathy, but
when she turns Christian any pity would be wasted on
her. She has gained a greater happiness than she has lost.
We shall therefore present Polyeucte and Pauline to
Hegel as characters who are too noble for our pity, and
we shall be content with our 'country cousin', Sévère. But
Sévère is a sceptic. *Tragédie Chrétienne* is a possible description of the play only if we keep the two words apart.
Where it is Christian, it is not tragic; and where it is
tragic, it is not Christian.

Few people would now claim for Corneille, and I suppose

[1] *Tragedy*, p. 110.

nobody would claim for *Samson Agonistes*, the qualities of great tragic drama. With Racine it is a different story. For those brought up on the Classics and on English literature, it is easy to say, with Macneile Dixon, 'Twice only has tragedy flowered to full perfection, once in Periclean Athens and again in Elizabethan England. The great tragic artists of the world are four, and three of them are Greek'.[1] I think that an unprejudiced judgement must allow Racine to join this select company. Perhaps Ibsen, too, but no question of religious Tragedy arises with him. Racine wrote two plays on religious themes, *Esther* and *Athalie*; and the last of his secular dramas, *Phèdre*, was claimed by him, and allowed by Port-Royal, to be conformable to Christian doctrine.

I take it for granted that *Esther* is not a Tragedy. It follows closely the Biblical narrative, in which the *peripeteia* is an uplifting of the good and a casting down of the wicked. Everyone will agree with Aristotle[2] that this kind of plot does not produce the tragic emotions.

The plot of *Athalie* follows the same conventional pattern of 'poetic justice'. The wicked Athalie and her priest of Baal are killed; young Joas, who has been saved from death and brought up as a model of virtue, is crowned king to continue the line of David. At first sight, therefore, there is nothing tragic in the plot. *Athalie* has been praised by many critics, including Voltaire and Sainte-Beuve, in the highest terms. It seems to me that the aesthetic appeal of the play lies chiefly in the quality of its poetry; and, as elsewhere in Racine, the characterization is impressive. I should not rate so high the *tragic* effect of the piece, but I think that it does make some

[1] *Tragedy*, p. 23.
[2] *Poetics*, xiii.

appeal to the tragic emotions. Athalie, though presented
for the most part as simply hateful, gains our sympathy
when she wavers between the counsel of prudence that
she should kill young Joas and the affection which his
appearance and character stir in her. In the end she
reaches a properly tragic grandeur with her final speech
before she is led out to execution. Acknowledging her
defeat by the God of the Hebrews, she yet defies him
with the prediction that the young king will grow up to
revolt against God and follow her own paths. I do not
think that any of the other characters is, properly speaking, a tragic hero. Joad the High Priest is heroic but not
tragic. He, too, prophesies future doom, but at once sees
this followed by the New Jerusalem. Joas, troubled by the
intimations of Athalie and Joad that he may go wrong, is
an object of pity to the audience, who know the future;
but he is, I think, too young to be heroic. At the same
time there is genuine tragic irony in the raising of pity at
the moment of his triumphant coronation.

Supposing that these remarks are justified, let us consider whether Racine's achievement in this play bears
out the contention that religious Tragedy (in the Biblical
sense of 'religious') is impossible. The thesis is borne out
by Racine's success in making Athalie herself strike the
tragic note. From the pagan point of view, it is proper
that Athalie, defeated by the power of a hostile God,
should stir pity for her fate and admiration for her defiance. From the Jewish or Christian point of view, the
pity is appropriate, but the admiration for her defiance
of God is impious. On the other side, the impending tragedy
of Joas and Jerusalem, foretold by the Hebrew High
Priest and lamented by the Chorus of Levites, is light-
ened by the glories of the New Jerusalem to follow; the

final note is therefore one of hope. This is illustrated particularly in the Choric Odes (Act III, scene viii) that follow Joad's prophecies. The Chorus begin with forebodings of doom, followed by perplexity at the double prophecy of evil and good. Here Racine strikes the authentic chord of Greek Tragedy. But at the close of the scene the Chorus end, as in a Biblical play they must, with faith in God that quiets their fears and gives them joy. There are Choric Odes in Greek Tragedy where the Chorus will end a song of fear and foreboding with a pious expression of hope that all will be for the best; but such expression is 'pious' in the pejorative sense of the word. A Greek Chorus in such circumstances does not really believe that things are going to turn out well, and the audience know that their hopes are futile. In the scene of *Athalie*, the Chorus of Levites have genuine faith in the justice and goodness of God, and the audience are expected to know that the fall of Jerusalem will be a just punishment for sin, that it is intended to do good, and that it will be followed eventually by a 'happy ever after'. On the whole, therefore, I think one must conclude that there is dissonance between the Biblical and the tragic notes in this play. Where Racine strikes the one, he misses the other. Yet it is remarkable how near he comes to harmony in the total aesthetic effect.

Phèdre illustrates even better Racine's genius for approaching a union of incompatibles. Here, too, he tries to fuse Greek Tragedy with Christian doctrine, but this time using a pagan and not a Biblical theme. Although Euripides' *Hippolytus* is his chief model, the character of his heroine is drawn from Jansenism. The voice is the voice of Phaedra, but the thoughts are the thoughts of

63

Port-Royal. When Phèdre speaks of Venus, the pagan goddess becomes the demon of Original Sin:

> *Ce n'est plus une ardeur dans mes veines cachée:*
> *C'est Vénus toute entière à sa proie attachée.*
> *J'ai conçu pour mon crime une juste terreur;*
> *J'ai pris la vie en haine, at ma flamme en horreur.*

A more subtle creation than Athalie, Phèdre is pagan and Christian together. Conscious of sin, she cannot avoid it, a victim at once of Greek fate and Jansenist predestination.

But can Racine combine in his audience the feelings appropriate to Greek Tragedy and those appropriate to Original Sin? He says in his Preface that the intention of the play is to show up vice and make us hate it. Phèdre would not be a great tragic character if our reaction were hatred. No doubt the malevolence theory of tragic pleasure, held by Rousseau and Émile Faguet, would allow Racine to say that our aesthetic satisfaction is bound up with hate of this damned soul in torment. Mr F. L. Lucas[1] compares Rousseau with those early Fathers who included among celestial pleasures the spectacle, *du paradis*, of the torments of hell. Whatever one may think of such a theatre in the after-life, we fortunately know that Racine's views of the mundane theatre in Athens and Paris were rather different. In the Preface to *Phèdre*, he says that the true purpose of Tragedy is not to divert but to instruct, and that the pursuit of such an aim might reconcile the religious to this form of profane drama. He also says, following Aristotle, that the tragic hero should have qualities exciting compassion and terror, and he explains why he thinks that the character of Phèdre satisfies Aristotle's rules:

[1] *Tragedy*, pp. 37–8.

'Phèdre is neither completely guilty nor completely innocent. She is involved by her destiny, and by the anger of the gods, in an illegitimate passion, which she more than anyone regards with horror. She does all she can to overcome it. . . . Her crime is a punishment from the gods rather than an act of will.'

In that case, one may well ask how on earth Phèdre can be regarded as a sinner, or her fate as just. If her *crime* is a 'punishment' from the gods, justice is indeed a blind goddess. In the death of Hippolyte, divine justice appears even more unjust. In order that Hippolyte's death should not cause 'more indignation than pity', says Racine, he has made Hippolyte subject to *'quelque faiblesse'* (our old friend *hamartia*), which would 'make him a little guilty towards his father'. The *faiblesse* is Hippolyte's love for a girl related to his father's enemies. For this, he is torn to pieces by a sea monster. As Racine says, 'the smallest faults are severely punished' in his play. This is the moral instruction that is to reconcile tragic drama with religion. It reminds me of the late Mr J. S. Smart's description of the doctrine of Gervinus, that in Shakespeare's eyes any fault is punishable by death. Macbeth murders a king; he must die. Desdemona shocks her father by marrying a blackamoor; she must die. Juliet imprudently allows herself to fall in love at first sight; she must die. 'Compared with this procedure, the Bloody Assize was humane', comments Mr Smart:

'If a man were brought before a criminal court, accused of stealing a box of matches, duly convicted of stealing a box of matches, and then sentenced to penal servitude for life, the public mind would be outraged:

such a penalty would seem to show a deeper guilt in the judge than in the culprit.'[1]

I do not know that the fate of Racine's Hippolyte stirs either indignation or pity, for the character is a dramatic failure. But in his portrayal of Phèdre, Racine undoubtedly reaches tragic sublimity. And like Lear, Phèdre is more sinned against than sinning. How could Racine suppose that the morality of his play would commend itself to the religious? Even more surprising, at first sight, is the assent of his spiritual mentors to that supposition.

Racine did not write the Preface to *Phèdre* with his tongue in his cheek. The form of religion to which he commended his drama was Jansenism. According to that doctrine, if Phèdre and Hippolyte be supposed to lack the arbitrary gift of divine grace, then indeed their smallest faults must carry the severest of penalties.

Ainsi que la vertu, le crime a ses degrés,

says Hippolyte. But there are no degrees of divine reward and punishment. Eternal bliss or eternal damnation, according as one is lucky or unlucky. Boileau writes of

la douleur vertueuse
De Phèdre malgré soi perfide, incestueuse.

No matter. She is predestined to sin and damnation. Predestination is sufficiently like the *Moira* of Greek myth to allow the existence of undeserved calamity.

But this is not quite the same as allowing the existence of Tragedy. I said of Athalie that a Christian standpoint allows pity for her fate but not admiration for her defiance of God. Phèdre does not defy God, and Christianity as

[1] J. S. Smart, 'Tragedy', in *Essays and Studies of the English Association*, Vol. VIII, Oxford: Clarendon Press, 1922, p. 25.

ordinarily understood would certainly grant admiration
for the effort to avoid sin. But this is assuming that the
avoidance of sin accords universally with God's purpose.
On a doctrine of predestination, can this be said? I am not
clear that it can. Can Jansenism allow admiration for
futile efforts to escape what God has decreed? Can it even
allow pity for miserable sinners when we recall that their
sin and misery alike are divinely appointed? These sympathetic feelings would imply some measure of hostility
to the power that dooms the sinner. Voluntary submission
to the divine order forbids the turning of sinners into
heroes. Racine does succeed, *malgré soi* perhaps, in making Phèdre a great tragic heroine, and he therefore fails
in the end to reconcile Tragedy with Christianity.

The extraordinary thing is that he should come so near
to it. He was able to do so because Christianity for him
meant Jansenism. Some people think it a mistake to talk
of Jansenism in connection with *Phèdre*. They may be
right, but if so the incompatibility of the Tragedy with
Christianity simply becomes more obvious and of a more
familiar kind. Libertarian forms of Christianity can allow
both pity and admiration for Phèdre; but they have to
face the former, more evident, difficulty of cosmic injustice, and on that score Racine's play is as much in conflict with orthodox Christian theology as is its Euripidean
prototype. The fact is that Racine's play can appear to
unify Tragedy with Christianity precisely because the
doctrine of predestination by-passes the problem of divine
injustice. The doctrine of predestination, emphasizing
God's omnipotence, almost loses sight of his moral attributes. Divine justice, if there be such a thing at all on this
view, is completely incomprehensible to the human in-
telligence and cannot be interpreted by human ideas of

67

justice. This being so, it is possible to stage a conflict, as in Greek Tragedy, between divine power and human ideas of justice. But the conflict can be *tragic* only if the side of justice is allowed to win our sympathy, with the implication of antipathy to the power opposing it.

Of the examples I have considered, the Racine plays are the only ones that can with any plausibility be called Tragedy within the ambit of Biblical religion. I have argued that even there the tragic and the religious impulses are in conflict. If the kind of situation that can give rise to Tragedy is to be treated in the spirit of Biblical religion, the human hero is liable to be abased so that he ceases to be a hero. The sense of the tragic requires us to feel the sublimity of the hero even more than that of the power of necessity. In a famous Choric Ode, Sophocles writes:

> Wonders are many, and nothing is more wonderful than man. . . .
> Only from Death will his contrivance find no escape.[1]

The Greek word *deinos*, here translated 'wonderful', possesses two meanings, 'wonderful' and 'terrible'. It covers both my senses of the sublime. Man cannot escape his destiny, says Sophocles. Death, which is also *deinos*—dreadful, awesome—stands over him with invincible power. Yet 'nothing is more sublime than man'.

[1] *Antigone*, 332, 361.

II. Philosophical Drama

1

The Philosopher as Dramatist — Plato and the Greek Drama

THE first essay in this book deals with philosophical questions *about* one type of drama. In the second, I propose to consider some relationships between drama and a branch of philosophy itself. I am going to discuss ways in which serious drama can be a vehicle of moral philosophy.

I must make it quite clear at the outset that I do not believe it is the primary business of the dramatist to play the philosopher. The appeal of drama is first and foremost aesthetic. Philosophical drama, if it is good drama, is in the first place art, and only in the second place is it philosophy. If I speak here of the philosophy, this is not because I have forgotten the art.

At the same time, I do not accept a complete disjunction between the aesthetic value of literature and the kind of value that philosophy can have. I would say that the philosophical character of philosophical drama contributes to the total *aesthetic* effect—provided the play is properly integrated, a successful example of its *genre*. (The same goes for the philosophical novel, again if properly integrated.) Writers on aesthetics too often assume that the different arts, and different *genres* in a single art, all make the same kind of aesthetic appeal. Benedetto Croce, whom

I regard as the greatest of philosophers of art, takes this position. One of the consequences, for him, is that there can be nothing in common between art and philosophy; philosophy is a species of conceptual thought, while art is 'intuition', or expression of feeling, and therefore pre-conceptual. I believe that this view cannot be sustained for *literature*. The medium of literature is words, and words are not just heard but understood. Of course, the literary artist does not use words merely to express concepts; if he did, he would be no artist. He gives new uses to words, uses whose effect depends on the imagination rather than the intellect. In that way certainly his art differs from the scientific use of words. Still, he cannot cut out of his words the concepts already implicit in them. Some poets have tried to do so, relying purely on the auditory effect of the words they use. But then what they are after is not poetry at all, but a kind of music. Poetry, like music, depends on the sounds, but it differs from music in that its sounds are also words, sounds that have meaning.

It is significant that the old dispute in aesthetics about instruction and delight has been pretty well confined to the purpose of literature. It does not make sense (Plato notwithstanding) to suggest that the purpose of music is to edify, and only in very restricted contexts does it make sense for painting, sculpture, or architecture. Let me add, however, that in this well-worn controversy I am with the advocates of delight. I mention the dispute solely in order to illustrate the point that specific aesthetic questions arise for literature because it uses a medium based upon the medium of ordinary communication. I do not myself think that the aesthetic value of literature depends on any instruction it may happen to impart, and this is not what I have in mind when I speak of the philosophical character of a play contributing to its aesthetic effect. We can separate the aesthetic value of literature from any didactic value that it may have. But we cannot separate the aesthetic effect from the conceptual content of the medium employed. The conceptual content is essential to the medium. The literary artist produces his effect by adding musical attraction and fresh imaginative associations to the conventional meaning of the words, but the additions depend on what is already there. The aesthetic effect of *literary* art can only be produced by exercising the imagination in the medium of meaningful language.

There is a further reason for rejecting Croce's absolute distinction between art and philosophy. He assumes not only that the value of art can owe nothing to the intellect, but also that the value of philosophy is entirely different from aesthetic value, bare truth and no more. This is too simple a view of philosophy. We may dream of the goal of philosophy as a final truth at the bottom of the well, but it is a bottom that will not be reached until the end of days. There can be successful philosophy for all that. Philosophy that succeeds as philosophy has a particular kind of aesthetic interest as well as an intellectual interest. A philosophic theory, to be acceptable, must accord with facts and must be internally coherent; thus far it must satisfy tests of truth, necessary but rather pedestrian, and a theory that merely satisfies these tests will be trite and unexciting. To be distinguished, a philosophic theory must strike the imagination. Some philosophers can do this by brilliance of style or novelty of method; but these are not essential. What is essential is the presentation of familiar facts in a novel perspective. This is a strictly philosophical use of the imagination, yet it is aesthetic. Works of literature that invite the epithet 'philosophical' always include this as one element of their aesthetic appeal.

In France, philosophy and literature go hand in hand. Gabriel Marcel tells us in his Gifford Lectures[1] that his plays express his philosophical thought 'in its virgin state'. The philosophy of his rival, Jean-Paul Sartre, was doubtless a woman of the world before she trod the boards of the theatre. Sartre uses the medium of the drama and the novel in order to communicate to a wider public ideas that have already been offered to philosophers in the traditional decent obscurity of a dead jargon. Whatever the purpose, these contemporary French philosophers who write philosophical drama are following an old tradition, a tradition that goes back almost to the beginnings of western philosophy, at any rate of western moral philosophy.

Socrates is said to have brought philosophy down from the heavens to earth, from astronomy (and physical science in general) to the life of man. That is to say, he was the first philosopher to make moral philosophy his prime concern. He was the first Greek philosopher to do so—if our picture of earlier Greek philosophers contains only those thinkers who are commonly called the pre-Socratic philosophers. I want to suggest that Plato had a different picture. In Plato's eyes, the Socratic dialectic was akin to dramatic dialogue, and Socratic ethical doctrine akin to the moral teachings of the dramatists. If fifth-century Athens was the school of Hellas, the theatre of Dionysus was the school of Athens. And Greek schooling or education, as Professor Werner Jaeger has shown in his brilliant study,

[1] *The Mystery of Being*, Vol. I, London: Harvill, 1950, p. 22.

Paideia, was an all-embracing conception—religion, philosophy, morals, as well as the imparting of knowledge and the development of aesthetic appreciation. In fifth-century Athens, the serious drama was the main instrument of *paideia*, and that means, of the development of religion and morals as well as of art. If we recall the half-truth that Homer was 'the Bible of the Greeks'—a half-truth because Greek religion is only in principle analogous to Biblical religion—we may also recall Aeschylus' remark that his plays were all slices from the banquet of Homer.

When Plato in the *Republic* attacks the ethics and theology of the poets, most of his quotations are taken from Homer and Aeschylus, from the source of serious drama and from the most highly respected dramatist. Plato attacks poetry because poetry was so often treated as the moral educator. He speaks of 'the eulogists of Homer who declare that he has been the educator of Hellas' (606e). In Book I, Polemarchus had defended a traditional conception of justice or morality by appealing to the authority of the poet Simonides; and Socrates had ridiculed the conception derived from this source. 'It is certainly hard to distrust Simonides', he says with his accustomed irony, 'since Simonides was a wise (*sophos*) and godlike man'. In fact Simonides is a man of straw, and Plato soon links him with a far greater poet, to show that the traditional wisdom (*sophia*) of 'the educator of Hellas' is contemptible beside the new wisdom (*philosophia*) that Plato himself can supply. The thesis of Polemarchus and Simonides, he says, implies that the just man is a sort of thief; and one might gather this from Homer, too, he continues, since Homer praises one of his characters for being good at stealing and cheating. So much for the preliminary slap-

75

stick of Book I. When Plato comes, in Book II, to his explicit criticism of poetry, he wastes no time on small fry
like Simonides—it is no great achievement to produce
better wisdom than they—but turns at once to Hesiod and
Homer for examples of immoral theology.

Few, if any, Athenians of the fifth and fourth centuries
will have taken their theology and ethics from Homer.
The ancient beliefs had been reshaped by several agencies
—by political and social change, by the doctrines of the
mystery religions, and above all by the tragic dramatists.
Plato's attack on poetry as a false moral educator is funda-
mentally an attack on the tragic drama. This is really
clear enough from the way in which Plato develops his
criticism in Books II and III, but it is placed beyond any
doubt when Plato returns to the subject at the beginning
of Book X. There he refers back to the criticism of poetry
as a criticism of 'the tragedians and the rest of the imitative tribe' (595a), and says that Homer 'is the great cap-
tain and teacher of all that goodly band of tragic writers'
(595b). A little later he adds: 'We hear persons saying
that the tragedians, and Homer, who is at their head,
know all the arts and all things human, virtue as well as
vice, and divine things too' (598d). He has included
Homer in his indictment only because Homer was considered the forebear of tragic drama, the Old Testament
of the tradition of poetry as religious doctrine. Tragedy
was a New Testament. It continued the tradition of
poetry as *paideia*, but reformed religious and moral ideas
so as to give men a new way of looking at human life and
human endeavour in relation to the powers, natural and
supernatural, that govern the world. Aeschylus and Euripides in particular—if not Sophocles too—question old
beliefs and propound new moral and religious conceptions.

It is worth noting that when Plato does come to the indictment of these conceptions of the tragic drama, his quotations are mostly taken from Aeschylus. The obvious target for a conservative was Euripides. But baiting Euripides was old game, and Plato, for all his conservatism, felt deeply that what he had to say was new. So when he comes to criticize Tragedy, he leaves Euripides alone. His readers would be quite familiar with moral objections to Euripides. Plato goes deeper than Aristophanes, who thinks of Euripides as the danger to public morals but regards Aeschylus as the teacher of sound doctrine. Plato is not content to reform later Tragedy and return to Aeschylus. He rejects all Tragedy, and so he attacks its most revered practitioner.

We are apt to think of Plato's moralistic evaluation of poetry, and especially of tragic drama, as perverse. It would not have seemed so to his readers. Werner Jaeger writes in *Paideia* of 'the undisputed supremacy' of Tragedy over a whole century, of its 'domination' of the Athenian mind, as evidenced by remarks of the comic poets, 'who mirrored the ideas of their time with no thought of posterity. The men of that age never felt that the nature and influence of tragedy were purely and simply aesthetic. Its power over them was so vast that they held it responsible for the spirit of the whole state'. Only by realizing this, Jaeger says, can we understand why Plato attacks poetry in the way he does. It was the work of Aeschylus, Jaeger continues, that first brought into being the idea that serious drama should express 'the spirit of the state'. That was why people who deplored the decline in the standards of later Tragedy sighed for the great days of Aeschylus; why Aristophanes, in *The Frogs*, wanted to bring Aeschylus back from the dead 'as the only man (in the absence of a Platonic censorship) who could recall poetry to its true function'.[1] But it is not the purpose of Plato's censorship to recall poetry to the function that Aeschylus had exercised. Plato wants to oust poetry from that function, to replace poetry by philosophy. This is why he picks on Aeschylus, the paragon of Aristophanes, in finding examples of bad spiritual guidance.

There are more specific reasons why Plato should think of himself as taking the place of Aeschylus. The *Republic* is Plato's *Oresteia*. The *Oresteia* of Aeschylus and the *Republic* of Plato both put forward a new doctrine of Justice. In one way, Plato is just continuing Aeschylus' work of purifying moral ideas. But in another way he is directly opposed to the teaching of Aeschylus. Professor H. D. F. Kitto, in a fascinating book, *Form and Meaning in Drama*, has pointed out that the *Oresteia*, like the Prometheus trilogy, expounds a theology of development, no less than an ethics of development, and that the idea of a progressing Zeus is a universalized picture of political progress, progress that had reached its highest point in contemporary Athens. 'We may remind ourselves', says Professor Kitto, 'that such a Polis which had come to witness the *Oresteia* was a relatively new thing in human history: it was the summit, so far, of human achievement: spiritual, moral, intellectual, political'.[2] In the *Oresteia*, Aeschylus is telling the Athenians that they are the salt of the earth. For Plato, the Attic salt had lost its savour. The political development that had culminated in Athenian democracy was, to Plato, a process of decline. In the beginning was the Good. Thereafter it could always be

---

[1] *Paideia* (translated by Gilbert Highet), Vol. I, Oxford: Blackwell, 1939, pp. 244–5.

[2] *Form and Meaning in Drama*, London: Methuen, 1956, p. 82.

said that there's a bad time coming. Change is always for
the worse. As for political justice, Plato thought, Athenian
democracy had none. Its vaunted liberty plucks justice by
the nose; and its proud boast of *isonomia*, equality before
the law, is an equal contempt for all laws. For justice, true
justice, we must go back to the older society that democracy destroyed. Plato's picture of democracy is a fierce
caricature of the funeral speech of Pericles, and his attack
on Tragedy is a bitter reproach of the poet who, in his
greatest work, had justified the recent Periclean reform
of the Areopagus that marked the end of the old aristo-
cratic constitution.

Yet Plato himself could not remain uninfluenced by the
power of Attic drama. I have already hinted that the dialogue form was suggested to Plato as much by the dialogue of drama as by Socrates' method of philosophic
inquiry. The 'irony' of Socrates, of which we hear in
Plato, is simply tragic irony in reverse. Tragic irony
arises from the self-deceit of the protagonist who thinks
he is wise while others know he is not. Socratic irony
arises from the self-knowledge of the protagonist who
knows he is wiser than others in being aware of his
ignorance.

These are not the only ways in which Plato learned
from the drama. It is well known that he admired the
Comedies of Aristophanes, and had a copy of them on his
deathbed. Many of the Socratic dialogues seem to me to
be essays in Philosophical Comedy. Socrates is the comic
hero, who seems less powerful than his adversaries but
manages to outwit them all, in dialogue that produces
instruction with laughter, just as in the Comedies of
Aristophanes. For Plato, Socrates was—in his life—a

comic hero surpassing any of the protagonists of Aristophanes. But this is of lesser importance than what Socrates was in his death. In his death Socrates was, for Plato, the supreme tragic hero.

And not only for Plato. Why is it that so many people compare Socrates with Jesus of Nazareth? It is largely because of Plato's *Phaedo*. I want to bring out a concealed factor in the *Phaedo* that contributes to the comparison. For this purpose, we shall need to return for a few minutes to the question of 'religious Tragedy'.

In speaking of the relation between Tragedy and religion in the first essay, I discussed 'the suffering servant' of *Isaiah*, and I said that the message conveyed by Isaiah is not tragic. Many Christians interpret the passage as a foreshadowing of the Crucifixion; and I suggested, when speaking of Cordelia in *King Lear*, that the account of the Crucifixion would be tragic for a pagan but cannot be so when read in the light of Christian theology. Throughout my discussion of Tragedy and religion I talked, in general, of 'Biblical theology'; and I think that was fair enough, despite the fact that Christian theology is more complex than Jewish. The greater complexity of Christian theology does not lessen the difficulty of creating religious Tragedy, since the Christian must accept the commitments of Hebrew theology as well as additional ones. The added complexity simply makes it less *apparent* that situations which are tragic on the surface cannot be so when interpreted in the light of theological requirements. The suggestion that the Crucifixion is not tragic is a startling one at first sight. This is because, with one side of the mind, Christians look upon the Crucifixion in purely human terms. Yet they cannot, as Christians, regard it solely on that plane.

At the same time, this two-sidedness of outlook is an essential factor in Christianity, which juxtaposes the optimistic doctrine of Hebraism and the tragic spirit of Hellenism. I have been led to see this by some comments of Rabbi Dr Ignaz Maybaum about a radio talk of mine in which I outlined the difficulties that lie in the way of religious Tragedy. I cannot do better at this point than quote some of his words:

'Christianity, which brought the good tidings to the Graeco-Roman world, had to speak to gentiles to whom tragic end meant noble fulfilment. The story of the Servant of God of whom we read in the Book of Isaiah is told in the Crucifixion as tragedy. This Christianised tragedy is no longer the pagan tragedy, neither is it the prophetic message of the good life.'[1]

He goes on to say, of the servant of God in *Isaiah*, that 'the story of a prophet's martyrdom is told as a success-story', since the servant is to 'succeed', 'be exalted and extolled, and be very high'. Dr Maybaum also contrasts the Christian tradition of speaking of 'the sacrifice of Isaac' with the Jewish one of speaking of 'the binding of Isaac', which emphasizes the fact that Isaac was not sacrificed. (It is, of course, relevant to relate the Crucifixion to the story of Abraham and Isaac, as well as to 'the suffering servant', since God's words to Abraham, 'Take now thy son, thine only son', are clearly recalled in the New Testament when God is said to have given 'his only begotten Son' to save the world.)

An important difference between Judaism and Christianity is indicated here, and I should agree that the

[1] Letter in the British Broadcasting Corporation's journal, *The Listener*, September 23, 1954, p. 489.

message conveyed by the Crucifixion is not the same as the prophetic message. Nevertheless, I do not agree that the new message is tragic. It is still a message of 'good tidings'; and for Christians, the martyrdom of Jesus has to be regarded as the accomplishment, not the frustration, of his mission—even perhaps (to use Dr Maybaum's phrase) as 'a success-story', however strange this seems at first, just as it did originally to the disciples.

But although I should deny that the new form of statement is tragic, it undoubtedly is a *new* form, one that includes, and transmutes, what was contained in the tragic form. In this sense one may speak, if one wishes, of a new form of 'Tragedy', which might be called 'salvational Tragedy'—so long as we remember that this implies that it is not really, but only seems, tragic. Now is not this precisely what Plato has produced in the *Phaedo*? The Socrates of the *Phaedo* is indeed a pattern, to that extent, of the Jesus of the Gospels, and has consequently made a similar impression on such readers as would not find the comparison blasphemous.

The *Phaedo* is a Philosophical Tragedy. It not only has the superficial *theme* of Tragedy, the death of a hero, 'the wisest, the most virtuous, and the best, of all the men of that time'. It has the *form* of tragic drama in all sorts of details. There is a 'prologue', set outside the action itself, and 'episodes' or 'acts' of dialogue on a great subject, interrupted twice by intervals of flash-back to the 'Chorus', one member of whom has seen, while the other now listens to, the drama of the death of Socrates. In these 'choric' intervals, comments are made expressing the feelings that the action of the drama is expected to induce in the 'audience'. This is one of the stock functions of the Chorus in Greek Tragedy. Let me quote one of the passages in the *Phaedo* that illustrate it. At a critical point in the narrative, the point where powerful objections have been presented to Socrates' initial argument for immortality, Phaedo stops to reflect on their emotional effect:

'All of us, as we afterwards remarked to one another, had an unpleasant feeling at hearing them say this. When we had been so firmly convinced before, now to have our faith shaken seemed to introduce a confusion and uncertainty, not only into the previous argument, but into any future one; either we were not good judges, or there were no real grounds of belief.'

Then Echecrates, who has been listening silently to Phaedo for a long time, breaks in and says:

'There I feel with you—indeed I do, Phaedo, and when you were speaking, I was beginning to ask myself the same question: What argument can I ever trust again? For what could be more convincing than the argument of Socrates, which has now fallen into discredit?'[1]

The argument itself (and we may recall that the prefatory summary of an ancient drama is called *hypothesis* in Greek and *argumentum* in Latin) takes an unusually dramatic form; at the end of each 'act', the participants are lifted to heights of exhilaration or (with the exception of Socrates himself) plunged into gloom. The soaring passages could almost be said to fulfil another function of the Chorus in a Greek tragic drama (though here they are given to the chief character), the function of singing a hymn to excite appropriate feelings. In these

[1] 88c-d. Jowett's translation.

83

passages, Socrates sings—there is no other word for it; this is his swan song—praises of the spiritual life and its benefits. They can lead a scholar like Sir Richard Livingstone to say:

'It is wrong to suppose, as most readers do, that the interest of the *Phaedo* lies in the arguments for immortality. Its true subject is the ideal of the spiritual life; its permanent value is its picture of this and the passionate plea of Socrates that men should live the life of the spirit on earth and so become capable of living it hereafter.'[1]

In the text of the dialogue, which he introduces in these terms, Sir Richard goes so far as to print in smaller type the more intricate parts of the philosophical discussion, including the only arguments that deserve to be treated seriously, namely the objections of, and the replies to, Simmias and Cebes. Of so little importance can the strictly philosophical aspect of the book be made to appear by the form and theme of the tragic drama.

In calling the *Phaedo* a tragic drama, am I reading into it a fancy of my own invention? I think there is clear evidence that Plato himself intended the dialogue to be read as a Tragedy, but a Platonic Tragedy, devoid of what Plato considered the defects of tragic drama. Right at the beginning, in what I call the prologue, Phaedo says this:

'I remember the strange feeling which came over me at being with him. For I could hardly believe that I was present at the death of a friend, and therefore *I did not pity him*, Echecrates; his mien and his language were so noble and fearless in the hour of death that to me he

---

[1] *Portrait of Socrates*, Oxford: Clarendon Press, 1938, p. 73.

appeared blessed (*eudaimon*). I thought that in going to the other world he could not be without *a divine call*, and that he would be *happy*, if any man ever was, when he arrived there; and *therefore I did not pity him as might seem natural* at such a time. But neither could I feel the pleasure which I usually felt in philosophical discourse (for philosophy was the theme of which we spoke). *I was pleased and I was also pained*, because I knew that he was soon to die, and *this strange mixture of feeling* was shared by us all; we were laughing and weeping by turns.'[1]

Now Plato's rules for poetry, in Book III of the *Republic*, include these: men should not be made afraid of death, nor told that the life after death is gloomy and miserable. And in Book X (605c-e), he says that the pity which Tragedy inspires calls for 'the gravest of all the accusations' to be made against poetry; Tragedy makes us sympathize with grief and take pleasure in our sympathy. Phaedo does not pity Socrates, for Socrates himself is not grieved, and his death seems a blessing, not an evil. Nevertheless, Phaedo and all the others experience that 'strange mixture' of pleasure and pain which is peculiar to the appreciation of Tragedy. When Phaedo speaks of this, he might be thought to contradict his earlier statements that he did not experience pity. He says that he was pained because he 'knew that Socrates was soon to die', and at first sight this looks the same as the pain we feel at the death of any tragic hero. For Plato, however, there is a difference. What Plato objects to is *sympathy with the grief* of a tragic hero. Provided the hero is himself not grieved, nor thought to be unhappy, Plato has no

[1] 58e–59a. Jowett's translation. I have italicized expressions that illustrate my thesis.

objection to a *non-sympathetic* pain at the loss of a hero. It is surely significant that Phaedo goes out of his way, at the start of the work, to describe his emotions in terms that are bound to recall the effect of Tragedy, and to add (twice, to make sure the point is taken) that he was nevertheless free from that most reprehensible of feelings, pity.

There is one phrase, in the passage I have quoted, that suggests a slightly different interpretation. It is the last phrase of all: 'we were *laughing* and weeping by turns'. This suggests that Plato was writing a Tragedy *and a Comedy* at the same time. I think this was his intention elsewhere, and it may be that he interpreted his new, reformed Tragedy in that sense. For Tragedy ends unhappily, in the grief of death or some other disaster, while Comedy ends happily, in the joy of a wedding or some comparable highlight of human life. So when Plato wrote about death so as to make it seem an occasion of the highest happiness for the protagonist, he might well have thought that he was joining Tragedy and Comedy together to produce the perfect form of drama.

Plato, in my opinion, certainly believed that he could write both Tragedy and Comedy. When he made Socrates say, in the *Symposium* (223d), 'that the genius of Comedy was the same as that of Tragedy, and that the writer of Tragedy ought to be a writer of Comedy also', I believe he was thinking of himself. Commentators have asked why Plato appears to contradict the statement of the *Symposium* when he says in the *Republic* (395a) that the same man cannot write both Tragedy and Comedy. James Adam, in his edition of the *Republic*, suggests that in the *Symposium* Plato is speaking of the ideal dramatist, and in the *Republic* of the dramatists actually to be found in

Athens. To this I would only add that we are meant to understand that Plato himself is the ideal dramatist.[1]

One could say, for instance, that both the *Symposium* and the *Republic* themselves illustrate Plato's talent for Comedy and Tragedy alike. In the *Symposium*, he shows how well he can imitate the vein and style of Aristophanes the writer of Comedy and of Agathon the writer of Tragedy. More important, the dialogue combines wit and humour with high seriousness. In the *Republic*, Book I is a typical example of the Socratic dialogues that I have called Philosophical Comedies; the proud, supposedly wise Sophist is shown up by Socrates as a fool. The main body of the *Republic* is of course not tragic in the usual sense, any more than is the *Symposium*. The only work of Plato's that is tragic in any familiar sense is the *Phaedo* (unless we add the *Apology* and the *Crito* as the other two members of a 'tragic trilogy' on the death of Socrates). But the Greeks distinguished Tragedy from Comedy as being 'serious' (*spoudaios*) instead of playful; and the *Republic* in particular has the purpose which Plato ascribes to tragic drama, and which he thinks tragic drama has fulfilled perniciously, the purpose of teaching serious moral doctrine. In the *Laws* (VII, 817b) Plato himself says that the representation of the best form of life, such as he is making in his picture of the ideal state, is 'the most genuine Tragedy'. Plato would agree with Marcel

[1] Professor H. D. F. Kitto (*Form and Meaning in Drama*, p. 226) explains the discrepancy by emphasizing the word τέχνη in the *Symposium* passage, and taking it to imply that if poetic creation were the exercise of knowledge, instead of inspiration, then, and only then, would the poet be able to turn his hand to whichever form he chose. I do not find this suggestion convincing; but if it is correct, it too allows me to add a gloss, namely that Plato thought of his own work as the product of genuine knowledge and as therefore superior to poetry.

that drama can be philosophy 'in its virgin state'. But he would not allow that the drama of Athens was a wise virgin. Wisdom was the prerogative of the true philosophy, and that philosophy showed drama as it ought to be.

Plato was not the first to take over from Tragedy both the task of inculcating *paideia* and the form in which the lesson was to be cast. Thucydides had already done the same. If Plato wrote Philosophical Tragedy, Thucydides wrote Historical Tragedy. Thucydides explicitly sees history under a pattern. Unlike his predecessor Herodotus, who called his work Inquiry (*historië*), Thucydides described his own recital by an older concept (*syngraphe*) that connotes the imposition of form on events. It is a commonplace that the Peloponnesian War, and especially the Sicilian Expedition, take on, in the pages of Thucydides, the pattern of Tragedy. Whether or not Thucydides was conscious of this, it is another example of the influence of the tragic drama on the Athenian mind. For my part, I think Thucydides was quite conscious of the tragic pattern. For he, like Plato, adapted to his own needs not only the general pattern but also the linguistic form of the drama. His narrative is interspersed from time to time with long speeches, which do not pretend to be verbatim reports but are given as 'the kind of thing' that would have been said; these speeches are a deliberate stylistic device to express the attitudes of different groups in different circumstances. I think the idea of using the device was suggested to Thucydides by the drama. Why, look at that especially curious series of speeches, the 'Melian Dialogue'. This surely was suggested by the dialogue of drama. Indeed one might say that it was Thucydides' a tempt to include a piece of *stichomythia* (line-by-line

88

repartee) in his historical drama. At one point, the questions and rejoinders are not far from being literally single-line repartee, and the manner in which they follow on each other is precisely that of dramatic *stichomythia*:

'*Melians:* How, pray, could it be as good for us to serve as for you to rule?

Athenians: Because for you submission is the lesser evil, and for us your destruction is the lesser good.

Melians: So you would not allow us to be neutral, friends instead of enemies, but allies of neither side?

Athenians: No, for your enmity harms us less than your friendship, which would be to our subjects a sign of our weakness, while your hatred would be a sign of our power.'[1]

It was once fashionable to call Thucydides a scientific historian as contrasted with the unsystematic and supposedly credulous Herodotus. Later scholars learned a greater respect for Herodotus' methods of inquiry, and showed that they are in principle thoroughly scientific. It would be better to mark the contrast in Thucydides by calling Thucydides a *philosophic* historian. And in his work, as in Plato's, the philosophical purpose takes a form inherited from the drama. Tragic drama was the moral philosophy of fifth-century Athens.

[1] Book V, 92–5.

—◦❧❧◦—

The Dramatist as Philosopher

'TRAGIC drama was the moral philosophy of fifth-century Athens.' *Moral* philosophy. Is that what Gabriel Marcel means when he says, in *The Mystery of Being*, that his plays express his philosophy? He seems to suggest something different in a more explicit statement that he makes in an essay entitled 'On the Ontological Mystery'. There he writes: 'I remain convinced that it is in drama and through drama that metaphysical thought comes to grips with itself and defines itself *in concreto*'.[1] This seems a strange thing to say about *metaphysical* thought in general. It could hardly apply to the metaphysical theories of Aristotle, Descartes, Spinoza, Leibniz, Berkeley, or Hegel. In calling his own philosophy metaphysical, Marcel seems to think it is an example of metaphysics in the sense of ontology, because its chief task is to elucidate the nature of 'being'. But by the word 'being' he means personal being, what it is to be a person, to participate in human life—as contrasted with 'having', the possession and use of things. For Marcel, investigation into 'the mystery of being' is a search for self-knowledge. Furthermore, it is not a purely theoretical search. Marcel distinguishes a 'mystery' from a 'problem', because a problem is purely

[1] Cf. *The Philosophy of Existence* (translated by Manya Harari), London: Harvill, 1949, p. 15.

90

theoretical, something to be explained by analysis, while a 'mystery' cannot be so treated in a detached way. As Mr E. L. Allen puts it, a 'mystery', in Marcel's sense of the word, 'can only be dealt with by some appropriate change of attitude on our part. . . . I cannot merely study and explain a mystery, I have to do something about it'.[1] To talk of metaphysical mysteries is an un-Anglo-Saxon activity, especially if the term 'mystery' is used in a mystifying way. But we understand Marcel clearly enough when he says, in 1950, 'It seems to me today . . . that the keynote of my dramatic work is ethical'.[2] What Marcel calls metaphysics is a philosophy of man rather than a philosophy of nature, a philosophy of conduct rather than a philosophy of knowledge.

There is an old, and I think a sound, tradition in many Universities, which separates Moral or Practical Philosophy from other branches of the subject. The distinction is not only one of subject-matter, the first kind of philosophy theorizing about conduct and the second theorizing about knowledge and belief. Moral philosophy, as practised by philosophers of acknowledged eminence, has been advocacy as well as explanation. Marx betrayed a limited knowledge of philosophers when he said 'Philosophers have only tried to explain the world, but the important thing is to change it'. Like religious teachers, moral philosophers have been reformers, moralists as well as metaphysicians. Many of them, like some religious teachers, have indeed confined their preaching of reform to the heart of man, and have been content to take society and

---

[1] *Existentialism from Within*, London: Routledge, 1953, p. 155.
[2] Lecture on 'The Drama of the Soul in Exile' (translated by Rosalind Heywood), printed as Preface to *Three Plays: A Man of God; Ariadne; The Funeral Pyre*, London: Secker, 1952, pp. 33–4.

the world as the unchangeable scene in which man must strive to save his soul. To that extent Marx's statement has some point. Other philosophers, however, have tried to change society as well as—sometimes even instead of —changing human character. Plato was only the first, as he was also the greatest, of philosophers whose metaphysical theories were bound up with the preaching of social reform. But all moral philosophers of any eminence have preached reform of some kind, though not necessarily social reform. To regard their work as simply explanatory of the good life is to misunderstand their aims and their interests. When a man's chief interest lies in the good life, for the individual or for society, it is unlikely to be the cool, detached interest of mere curiosity. Hume's interest in morals may have had this character (though one might doubt it even in his case), but an interest in morals was not his dominant interest. Spinoza is at first sight the most scientifically-minded of all philosophers. He even interprets religion as science, identifying the worship of God with a delight in acquiring knowledge of Nature. Yet his greatest work, the most metaphysical of all metaphysics, is rightly entitled *Ethics*, and is, for all the cold, austere beauty of its geometrical form, as powerful a piece of philosophical preaching as can be found anywhere. If he interprets religion as science, he also interprets science as religion. To identify the object of religious worship with the object of scientific study is to make science religion as much as it is to make religion science. In singing the praises of the pursuit of natural knowledge, he advocates the attitude of the religious worshipper.

This is not to imply that moral philosophy is no different from sermonizing, that philosophical preaching is just preaching, any more than that religious teaching is just preaching. Theology is a brand of metaphysics; and in religion and moral philosophy alike, metaphysics is used to explain the preaching of a way of life. Needless to say, there are differences between moral philosophy and religion (in our western tradition, if not always in the east). Where the ultimate source of religious metaphysics is revelation, the kind of explanation it supplies is not that of the rational metaphysics of philosophers. Then, secondly, there is a difference in the proportions in which the preaching is mixed with the explanatory procedures of unifying and justifying the prescriptions espoused. If religious ethics is ninety per cent preaching to ten per cent theorizing, moral philosophy reverses the proportions. We find the philosophical function of unifying moral doctrine in some of the sayings of religious teachers; for instance in the Golden Rule, which is said to sum up the manifold prescriptions of the Mosaic Law. And we find the philosophical function of justifying moral doctrine in such verses as this: 'Be ye holy, *for* I the Lord your God am holy' (a theological or metaphysical justification); or this: 'And a stranger shalt thou not oppress; *for* ye know the heart of a stranger, seeing ye were strangers in the land of Egypt' (a psychological justification). Theological justifications are the more common type in the Bible, and since the theological dogmas to which they appeal rest on revelation, we may be disinclined to allow that they give any rational explanation. But they can also be regarded, as can some of the metaphysical 'explanations' of the Rationalistic philosopher, as repetitions, in a different form, of the moral doctrine they are supposed to 'explain'. Recasting a prescription in ostensibly descriptive language often has the psychological effect of calming doubts and quieting queries; and so it comes to be thought of as giving an explanation of what previously appeared to be a problem.

A metaphysical 'explanation' of ethics may take the form of giving a general description of an ideal state of affairs in which a recommended way of life is standard practice; and perhaps also a description of the very different state of affairs that results from neglecting to follow the recommended way of life. The relations between the several virtues are explained by attempting to assign to them related rôles in the general scheme. The description is general or abstract. A parable performs a similar function in *concrete* terms; it gives a picture of an imaginary situation in which particular individuals are faced with essentially the same choice as that confronting those who are addressed. Often the parable disguises the analogy by altering as much as possible the *inessential* features of the situation, in order that the identity of the underlying essential feature may stand out the more vividly. Theological language fuses the two methods by giving the abstract metaphysical description in terms of a personal God.

Serious drama is like the parable. It can manifest '*in concreto*' what moral philosophy treats in the abstract. Plato leads us from an inadequate definition of justice to a more adequate one by describing an ideal society, in which justice appears 'in larger letters'; Aeschylus feels his way towards an improved idea of justice by showing us a particular person in an intolerable dilemma caused by the claims of the old idea of justice. Where an Aristotle will discuss the difference between two kinds of vice in terms of abstract psychology, a Shakespeare will present us with Macbeth on the one hand and Iago on the other. As in the parable, the generality of the topic is disguised by making the characters highly individual, even improbable. We have all been faced with conflicting duties at one time and another, but never with such a dilemma as Orestes. We have all been tempted by ambition, but not to murder for the sake of a throne. Such stark and extraordinary examples, however, serve to bring out all the more vividly the force of the element that *is* the common lot of mankind. When Sophocles wishes to show the frailty of human knowledge amid the baleful vicissitudes of Fortune, he picks out Oedipus, whose extraordinary fate was almost matched by extraordinary intellect. Oedipus alone was able to solve the riddle of the Sphinx. Yet his talent, and his consequent urge, for finding out the truth, only contributed in the end to the horror of his misfortune. No one could ever be quite like Oedipus. But just because of that, there stands out more sharply the tragic irony of his confidence, a human weakness in an inhuman world. The moral issue is general; the method of presenting it is the parable, ' "metaphysics" defining itself *in concreto*'.

But the method is not just the simple parable. It is the *dramatic* parable, a more powerful medium. A narrator may tell the tale of good men and bad, perhaps with moralistic aim and effect. But in the drama, here they are before your eyes. They 'act'; the 'drama' *is* their action, for that is just what the Greek word means. The actor dons the mask (*persona*) of Oedipus; he speaks in the 'person' of Oedipus. As Plato says in the *Republic*, dramatic representation has a more powerful effect on the 'imitative' tendencies of the audience than has narrative description. If we read or hear about the fortunes and

95

misfortunes of a character in a novel or an epic poem, we shall appreciate what the author intends to convey, only if we exercise our imagination so as to feel ourselves into the place of the character or the place of those who have to do with him. But this *Einfühlung* through imagination is greatly facilitated when the character speaks and appears *in propria persona*. By being confronted with him, we are placed one stage nearer to those who confront him in an 'I-thou' relation. Sympathetic imagination of the feelings of other persons would be impossible for one who was not himself a person, engaged at some time in 'I-thou' relations with other persons. I can use my imagination to appreciate the experiences of people in a far-off land, or the experiences of those in far-off times, only because I appreciate, without any effort of imagination, the experiences of my neighbours whom I meet face to face. The extension of moral attitudes is facilitated when a parable represents a Samaritan, the stranger within the gates, as my neighbour, and even more when dramatic representation brings the stranger before my eyes.

At the same time, the dramatist uses additional devices to show up the universal character of what is presented *in concreto*. I said earlier that theological language fuses the abstract method of metaphysics with the concrete method of parable by expressing universal conceptions in personal terms. The dramatist does the same. If he writes in an age that finds a religious apperception of morality quite natural, the dramatist can use the concrete metaphysics of theology itself to aid him in universalizing the particular. Professor Kitto has shown, in *Form and Meaning in Drama*, how Aeschylus and Sophocles present the subject-matter of their Tragedies on a 'dual plane'. They give causal explanations of the action on two levels, human and divine, psychological and metaphysical. Cly-temnestra is motivated to murder by natural human emotions; but she is also the mere instrument of divine retribution, and her act a mere example of the cosmic law of Justice. 'The dual plane', writes Professor Kitto, 'universalizes the action. . . . It shows . . . that the action is not merely a particular event; it is a manifestation of Law. The dual plane generalizes it.'[1] The effect of the 'dual-plane' device can be achieved even if both planes refer to human existence. For instance, in *King Lear* the experiences of the king are repeated, as it were in shadow, by the experiences of Gloucester. One function of the repetition is to generalize the theme. It has other functions too, of course, notably to point a contrast as well as a similarity, like the reflection of Hamlet's task of revenge in that of Laertes. Doubling the image purely for the sake of throwing a shadow was left to mechanical hacks of a later age, parodied by Sheridan in *The Critic*, where Mr Puff's Elizabethan heroine, Tilburina, enters, 'according to custom', stark mad in white satin, accompanied by her confidant, stark mad in white linen.

The device, especially popular in the French theatre, of refurbishing the themes of ancient drama and history, is another method of employing the dual plane. Racine used classical themes to recall, but also to reshape, the Greek identification of psychological with divine causation. In the secular atmosphere of the twentieth century that is hardly possible (though Mr T. S. Eliot evidently persuades some people that it is). But Jean Giraudoux, wishing to talk about war and peace in the nineteen-thirties, universalizes his theme by making it take its theatrical shape in ancient Troy. And Jean-Paul Sartre,

[1] *Form and Meaning in Drama*, p. 74.

in *The Flies*, uses the old Greek story of Orestes to produce a dual plane twice over. This play is, I think, of particular interest for our present discussion.

In the first place, Sartre, like Giraudoux, speaks of contemporary political problems by representing an analogous situation in ancient Greece. So far as his political aim is concerned, however, the purpose of the dual-plane device is not so much to universalize the theme (of justifiable assassination) as to outwit the Nazi censor. The play was first produced during the occupation of France by the Germans in the Second World War. Sartre puts on the stage Aegistheus instead of a *Gauleiter*, a Chorus of Flies instead of occupation troops, Orestes instead of a member of the *maquis*. His audience took the point and enjoyed the trick. In this play Sartre justifies the Resistance, and its violent acts, before the very noses of its enemies. Two men come down from the hills to an occupied town, kill the Governor, and go off again pursued by the 'plague of flies'.

Secondly, the play has a philosophical significance as well, and here the dual plane does have the purpose of universalization. Like Euripides, Sartre turns an old myth to his own use in order to question traditional ideas of religion and morality. When Zeus speaks of what is pleasing to the gods, the sentiments he expresses are those that Sartre tendentiously ascribes to conventional Christianity:

> Fear and guilty consciences have a good savour in the nostrils of the gods. Yes, the gods take pleasure in such poor souls.

Again, Zeus says to an old woman of Argos:

> Try to earn forgiveness by repenting of your sins. . . . Be sure you die in a nice bitchy odour of repentance. It's your one

hope of salvation. Unless I'm much mistaken, my masters, we have there the real thing, the good old piety of yore, rooted in terror.

Later, when Aegistheus tells Zeus that the people of Argos fear him, Zeus replies:

Excellent! I've no use for love.[1]

So much for Sartre's critical purpose. He also has a positive thesis, and he uses the old myth to expound the ethics and metaphysics of Existentialism as an improvement on conventional ethics and religion (as he interprets them). The people of Argos are inauthentic men, enslaved by superstition and habit. Orestes' tutor has rid himself of that nonsense, but he is a sceptic, a typical old-style philosopher, unwilling to commit himself to anything. Orestes has been weaned by him from conventional beliefs to philosophical scepticism. But the critical situation turns Orestes into an Existentialist, an authentic man who accepts freedom and the responsibility of an act that convention calls wicked. He accepts the burden of responsibility, but not the crushing burden of repentance. Electra shows how easy it is to slip back into inauthentic existence. She had rebelled against the mumbo-jumbo of the prevailing superstition, but when the murder is done she is beguiled by the force of tradition (represented by Zeus) into repentance, and thereby she turns into a replica of Clytemnestra.

How much more vivid and arresting this is than the exposition of Existentialism in the usual philosophical jargon. The play's the thing wherein to catch the conscience.

[1] *Two Plays : The Flies; In Camera* (translated by G. Stuart), London: H. Hamilton, 1946, pp. 17, 14, 68.

'To catch the conscience.' But is that doing moral *philosophy*? I admit that the term needs some further justification. What, after all, have I shown so far? First, that moral philosophers can be, and that the eminent moral philosophers of the past were, moralists; and secondly, that many dramatists (including the Greek tragedians) have been moralists. But this is no news. Everybody knows that serious dramatists, like a good many writers in other forms of literature, tend to be moralists. As for philosophers, everyone knows that many of them too, in the past, have tended to be moralists. But moralizing does not make a writer into a philosopher (except in a popular sense of the word), and some philosophers today tell us that the philosophical work of classical philosophers should be distinguished from their moralizing. What else have I shown? That Plato (like Thucydides) was influenced by tragic drama not only in having a moralistic purpose but also in the form he gave to his work. But this is just a historical fact about one philosopher, and does not seem relevant to the general distinction between the philosopher and the moralist. One philosophic swallow may make an Indian summer for Greek Tragedy, but cannot dispel the winter of our discontent with moralizing philosophers.

Well, what is the distinction between the philosopher and the moralist? We shall all agree that the mark of the philosopher is to use rational methods of persuasion, logic. Logic is the tool of philosophy. Are we to go farther and say that logic is his sole subject-matter? This is a fashionable dogma in some quarters today. The philosopher's proper business, it is said, is to examine and elucidate methods of argument. I need not say that I do not regard the dramatist as a logician. But I do not regard the moral philosopher as a logician either. To study the logic of moral reasoning is certainly one proper task for a philosopher, but it is a *logician's* task. Although many moral philosophers have also been logicians, their examination of logic is not what constitutes their ethical theorizing. Ethical theorizing uses arguments and criticizes counterarguments in order to establish or question positions. It may examine, *en passant*, what makes such arguments sound or unsound, but that is not its primary business.

In contrasting the moral philosopher with the logician, am I identifying the moral philosopher with the moralist? That depends on what we understand by the word 'moralist'. If the moralist is taken to be one who moralizes or preaches virtue, then I must repeat what I said before, that the work of the great moral philosophers is only ten per cent preaching to ninety per cent theorizing. The main task of the moral philosopher, in my view, is to unify and to justify moral precepts and attitudes. Justification of course implies criticism too. Some philosophers will justify commonly accepted precepts. Others will criticize the accepted precepts and, in the light of their criticism, propose new views or at least modifications of the old. All these functions call for rational procedures, the *use* of logic. But all of them also have a practical bearing, and if the word 'moralist' is thought to convey, more than the word 'philosopher', a practical concern with moral questions, I am quite content to call the moral philosopher a moralist.

What we need to ask now is whether the dramatist is a moralist in the one sense or the other. There is no doubt that plenty of dramatists have been preachers, propagandists. But the propaganda play is not often a great play. The propagandist is sure of himself. He knows what he wants to advocate as well as what he wants to criticize. This is not, on the whole, true of those dramatists that we call great. They often know what they want to criticize. They raise questions and doubts about things that their audience have been inclined to take for granted; and in this respect their work is like that of critical philosophy. When it comes to putting forward positive views in place of those that have been questioned, great dramatists are, I think, much more hesitant than philosophers, much less sure of themselves. Their work may *suggest* to us a more appropriate attitude, but no more. Mr Geoffrey Brereton, in a radio talk on Tragedy,[1] has said that tragic drama 'can be seen as an ethical exploration . . . an exploration and not a demonstration', and he added that this kind of drama must be distinguished from the didactic. Likewise there is exploratory moral philosophy and didactic moral philosophy. The exploratory philosopher, more often than the exploratory dramatist, feels that he has discovered what he seeks, and so becomes didactic, too; but it is his exploration that is the more impressive philosophically.

Marcel, undoubtedly, would approve these sentiments. His conception of philosophy is certainly one of exploration, seeking to know oneself, to strip off skin after skin of illusion, in the hope of finding the core of real self within—in the hope, but without any confidence that it will be found, or even perhaps that it is there to be found. In the lecture to which I referred earlier, Marcel speaks scornfully of 'that type of philosophical drama' which expresses 'thought which has been thought al-

[1] 'The Hidden God: Some comments on the problem of Tragedy', broadcast in the Third Programme of the British Broadcasting Corporation on January 29, 1957. The BBC has kindly provided me with a copy of the text.

ready' instead of 'thought in the process of being thought'.
By 'that type of philosophical drama' he evidently means
the plays of Sartre, and he deplores the 'woeful misconception' whereby he has been taken to be an advocate of
a philosophy akin to Sartre's, 'whereas in fact', he says,
'I have always been its most determined opponent'.[1]
I should perhaps add, in case my quotation should lead to
any 'woeful misconception' about my own opinion, that,
judging by the few plays of Sartre and Marcel that I know,
I think Sartre is the better dramatist—and only in some
respects the weaker philosopher. I should not call either of
them a great dramatist or a great philosopher, but since
they are both explicit philosopher-dramatists of our own
time, it is interesting to observe that they exemplify the
two types of the exploratory and the cocksure thinker.

Let me now mention a modern play which I think does
have some claim to greatness, Arthur Miller's *The Crucible*. One hears it said that this was meant to be a propaganda play, castigating the 'witch-hunts' of the McCarthy
era by pointing to parallels in the witch-hunt at Salem
two and a half centuries before. There seems to be no
doubt that Arthur Miller did have this purpose in mind,
at least when he edited the play for publication, since
several of the notes which interrupt the text explicitly
indicate modern parallels. In the play itself, however, the
genius of the dramatist swamps the motives of the propagandist. A person who saw this play and had not been told
of its propagandist purpose would probably not think of
modern witch-hunting specifically. Of course he would
not be confined to the seventeenth-century scene either.
He would see in the play something of universal import,

[1] Preface to *Three Plays : A Man of God; Ariadne; The Funeral
Pyre*, p. 14.

as one sees in any play that touches greatness. He would see an exploration of the nature of human goodness and human evil, of how evil grows from things like envy and sexual frustration, *aided* by socially conditioned attitudes such as bigotry and superstition. He would see how the spread of this evil can bring calumny and death to innocent and even to saintly people. But he would also see how it can bring out, in a man who is no saint, goodness that might otherwise have remained merely potential.

Until we reach the end of the play, John Proctor is not a particularly good man. He can succumb to temptation as well as stand up for decency. His virtue is honesty. He is honest above all with himself. So when he is faced with the alternatives of death on a false charge and escaping death by a false confession, the decision is not clear cut for him, as it would be for the single-minded virtue of his wife, and as it is for the saintly character of Rebecca Nurse. He wrestles with his conscience, debating whether it would not be more dishonest for him to withhold the lie than to tell it. Up to now he has refused to 'confess' to sorcery, but he has no illusions about his reasons:

> Spite only keeps me silent. It is hard to give a lie to dogs.

If he now gives them the lie they want, it will not deceive anyone who is not already self-deceived. It would be more deceitful for him to play the martyr:

> I'd have you see some honesty in it. Let them that never lied die now to keep their souls. It is pretence for me, a vanity that will not blind God nor keep my children out of the wind. . . . I think it is honest, I think so; I am no saint. Let Rebecca go like a saint; for me it is fraud!

Yet in the end he tears up his confession, because he objects to his being used to incriminate others or to serve as an example of submission. So he joins Rebecca in martyrdom, but for a reason that is not false to his own humanistic code of conduct, and he can say of himself:

> Now I do think I see some shred of goodness in John Proctor. Not enough to weave a banner with, but white enough to keep it from such dogs.

But the last word, and the truest estimate of what he has achieved, is spoken by his wife, when he has left the stage and she is urged to go and plead with him to accept the lie:

> He have his goodness now. God forbid I take it from him.

In this play we have an impressive example of moral philosophy '*in concreto*'. Where the philosopher will give an abstract definition of different types of virtue, here we have them shown in living examples. And we also have, what we do not often find in philosophy, an exploration of the complex relations between moral good and moral evil. All this comes out more prominently than any propagandist purpose of censuring witch-hunting, ancient or modern. If it were otherwise, *The Crucible* would not be, as I think it undoubtedly is, by far the best of Arthur Miller's plays.

You will recall that when Mr Brereton described tragic drama as ethical exploration, he distinguished exploration from *demonstration*. This might suggest that the exploratory dramatist does not use the rational procedures of logic. If so, does not this mean that his work cannot be compared to philosophy, which must use the tool of logic? Not necessarily. The exploratory dramatist, like the exploratory philosopher, can still use rational procedures even though he does not demonstrate positive conclusions. Strict deduction is not the only kind of rational thinking.

As Mr Stuart Hampshire has written, 'One should never allow oneself to be intimidated by logicians. They cannot make the laws of argument; they can only codify them when they are already in force.'[1] If suggestive analogy carries conviction through standing the tests of criticism and experience, we call it rational.

Not that dramatic argument, any more than metaphysical argument, is devoid of strict deductive logic. What, after all, does deductive logic do? It serves to clarify positions, to show whether we are being consistent or inconsistent, no more. It is a great deal, but it is not everything; deductive reasoning cannot *create* a position. The dialogue of drama, like the dialectic of Socrates and the logical argument that developed from it, often serves to clarify positions, to show whether they are consistent or inconsistent.

This is especially true of *stichomythia* in the Greek drama. Aristophanes saw the point when he brought logic itself on the stage in *The Clouds*. One of the most delightful things in that play is the debate, beginning with some brisk *stichomythia*, between the logic of moral thinking and the logic of self-interest. But consider a piece of *stichomythia* in a serious play; for instance, this exchange between Antigone and Creon:

Cr: Have you no shame? No one else agrees with you.
An: There is nothing shameful in showing reverence to one's kin. [The others are not in my position of kinship to Polyneices.]
Cr: Well, was not Eteocles your kinsman, too?
An: He was, a brother born of the same father and the same mother.
Cr: Then why do you render a tribute impious in his eyes?

[1] 'Uncertainty in Politics', an article published in *Encounter*, January 1957.

106

An: Now that he is dead [and so likewise needs the tribute of burial], he will not call it so.

Cr: Yes he will, if your tribute to him is the same as to the impious.

An: No, for Polyneices was his brother, [an equal,] not a slave.

Cr: They were not equal. The one died invading this land, the other defending it.

An: Death [equalizes and] desires the same rites.

Cr: [I spoke of what Eteocles would desire.] The good man does not desire that he should receive the same treatment as the bad.

An: Who knows if these thoughts are approved among the dead?

Cr: Once an enemy, never a friend, even in death.

An: My nature is not to join in enmity but to join in love.

Cr: Then go to Hades and love the dead, if love you must. While I live, no woman shall rule me.[1]

The argument causes both characters to clarify their position, and to modify it, too. Up to the last speech of each, the points made are entirely logical. Creon tries to show Antigone that she is being inconsistent. Antigone denies it, first by opposing to Creon's premiss (that Eteocles would disapprove) the contrary proposition, then by the less radical but more secure proposition that neither of them is entitled to claim Eteocles' support. The final speech of each character is not a logical conclusion, but an expression of attitude. Yet these expressions of attitude can be put into words, and can be fully grasped by the speakers themselves, only because irrelevant points have been cleared out of the way by logic. Is not this thoroughly typical of philosophical argument?

Consider again this very short argument in Corneille's *Polyeucte.* Polyeucte, newly converted to Christianity, proposes to seek martyrdom; his fellow Christian, Néarque, tries to dissuade him:

[1] Sophocles, *Antigone,* 510–525.

107

Néarque: Vous voulez donc mourir?

Polyeucte: Vous aimez donc à vivre?

Néarque asks his question from the standpoint of the natural man: you cannot *want* to die. Polyeucte replies from the standpoint of a Christian: you cannot, as a Christian, be in love with *life*—and Néarque is silenced.

Logic is used, in drama as in philosophy and as in all thought, to secure consistency. If a position is found to be inconsistent, it is dropped. But neither philosophy nor life is satisfied with logic alone in testing a position. It must be able to stand up to experience too. Ethical positions in drama are tested by logic, in the dialogue, and by experience, in the action. In Sophocles' *Antigone*, the first words of Creon, after Antigone and Haemon have killed themselves, are: 'Alas, I have learned'. The practical consequences of his former stand have undermined its foundations.

I do not for a moment suggest that the particular pattern of relationship, which I traced between the Greek drama and the philosophy of Plato, is repeated in the drama and the moral philosophy of later days. Greek Tragedy performed the function of moral philosophy at a time when moral philosophy as such did not yet exist. Although many later dramatists are said to express a 'philosophy', they do not *initiate* philosophy in the way that the Greek tragedians did. (Marcel is perhaps an exception, if we are to take it that a self-consciously philosophic aim arose in him only after he had written some of his plays.) Sometimes, indeed, the Greek pattern is reversed, the dramatist taking over from the philosopher. Corneille uses the philosophy of Descartes, and Racine (to some extent) the philosophy of Jansenism. As for Shakespeare or

Molière, although they are as 'philosophic' as you like, it is virtually impossible, without presuppositions and forcing, to extract from them any one definite view of human life and the universe in which it is lived. Often enough they are *critics* of conventional conceptions; but so far as any positive substitute is concerned, they are the most tentative of explorers.

In Hegelian days, Hebbel could think of three great waves of philosophical drama—thesis, antithesis, synthesis—each performing the same sort of function, that of expressing the grand conflict of the age. Great drama, he thought, is brought to birth by a crisis in history, the transition from one form of civilization to another. Greek drama expresses the belief in fate that superseded earlier belief in the gods, and it depicts the conflict between man and 'the Idea'. The second great period of drama expresses the individualism of Protestant thought, and depicts the conflict within man himself. (Apparently the second great period of drama means Shakespeare, and Shakespeare, when you come down to it, means *Hamlet*.) The third great period was just coming, since a new form of civilization was just coming, and this third (and presumably final) type of drama was to express the conflict within 'the Idea' itself.[1] Well, you can see here how a man can build up a universal thesis on the evidence of Greek drama and one Shakespearean play. Professor Kitto, in his *Form and Meaning in Drama*, has also linked *Hamlet* with Greek Tragedy, but in the very different thesis that *Hamlet* belongs to the *same* form of 'religious drama' as was

[1] I am indebted, for the above account of Hebbel's views, to Eric Bentley, *The Playwright as Thinker*, New York: Meridian Books, 1955, p. 51. He explains that 'the Idea' means political, religious, and moral institutions.

written by Aeschylus and Sophocles. No doubt these suggestions are stimulating and add to our appreciation of *Hamlet*. But only a Hegelian would dare to generalize about the second great age of drama as a whole. It may be that the emergence of great drama is connected with a transition from one form of civilization to another. That is certainly true of great philosophy, at least in the history of western civilization. (Whether it is true of the drama and philosophy of other civilizations, I have no idea. Neither had Hebbel.) But I do not think we can usefully say that Shakespeare, Racine, and Molière (all of whom deserve the title of greatness) were doing the same sort of thing in the same sort of way.

Finally, I must repeat that I do not regard the great philosophical dramatists as having consciously set out to do a philosopher's job in their plays—as Shaw, Marcel, and Sartre have set out in our own day. Aeschylus and Sophocles did not think of themselves as philosophers, for the specific concept of philosophy did not then exist. (It seems to have been invented by Isocrates.) Quite apart from the concept, I should doubt whether they had a clear positive idea of preaching or explaining ethics and theology. Even Ibsen, of whom we naturally think as an explicit preacher of reform, is reported to have said: 'I was surprised that I, who had made it my chief task in life to depict human characters and human destinies, should, without conscious intention, have arrived in several matters at the same conclusions as the social-democratic moral philosophers'.[1] In intention Ibsen was an artist, as was Aeschylus. Nevertheless they both produced moral philosophy as well as great drama.

I have confined myself to drama. It is obvious enough

[1] Quoted from Eric Bentley, *The Playwright as Thinker*, p. 129.

that other forms of literature can similarly be the vehicle of philosophic thought. Today one thinks especially of the novel, since the form of the novel is the most congenial medium of literary expression for our present age; it has become so plastic that it seems able to take the place of nearly all the different literary *genres* of the past. I have tried to show that the drama has had one or two peculiar advantages for the particular purpose of conveying moral thought. However that may be, moral philosophy does well to associate itself with living literature, as the philosophy of knowledge does well to associate itself with living science. We may smile at the erstwhile vogue of Sartre in 'Existentialist night-clubs' among people who read his novels and saw his plays but who would not have understood a word of his strictly philosophical books. But Sartre is entitled to smile more broadly at a philosophy that is confined to articles in learned journals. Philosophy that lives alone is soon left alone.

INDEX OF AUTHORS CITED